MW00386850

GOSPEL

Recovering the Power of Christianity

JDGREEAR

Bible Study Developed by
SPENCE SHELTON

LifeWay Press® • Nashville, Tennessee

Spence Shelton
Writer

Joel Polk
Editorial Team Leader

Reid Patton, Brian Gass
Content Editors

Brian Daniel
Manager, Short-Term Discipleship

David Haney
Production Editor

Michael Kelley
*Director, Discipleship
and Groups Ministry*

Jon Rodda
Art Director

Published by LifeWay Press® • © 2011 J. D. Greear • Revised 2018 • Reprinted 2018

Previously published as *Gospel Revolution*

ISBN 978-1-5359-2566-2 • Item 005808004

Dewey decimal classification: 248.84

Subject headings: DISCIPLESHIP \ CHRISTIAN LIFE \ BIBLE—N.T. GOSPELS

To order additional copies of this resource, write to LifeWay Resources Customer Service; One LifeWay Plaza; Nashville, TN 37234; email orderentry@lifeway.com; fax 615-251-5933; phone toll free 800-458-2772; order online at LifeWay.com; or visit the LifeWay Christian Store serving you.

Printed in the United States of America

Groups Ministry Publishing • LifeWay Resources • One LifeWay Plaza • Nashville, TN 37234

CONTENTS

About the Author

At the age of twenty-seven, **J. D. Greear** became the pastor of a forty-year-old neighborhood church. In the years since, that congregation of four hundred has grown to more than five thousand in weekly attendance. Today the Summit Church, located in Raleigh-Durham, North Carolina, is one of the fastest-growing churches in North America.

J. D.'s messages aren't intended just to show people how to live better lives. His goal is to leave people in awe of God's amazing love. Because of his belief in the power of the gospel, J. D. has led the Summit to set a goal of planting more than one thousand gospel-centered churches in the next forty years.

J. D. holds a PhD in systematic theology from Southeastern Baptist Theological Seminary. He also lived and worked among Muslims in Southeast Asia for two years and wrote *Breaking the Islam Code*. J. D. and his beautiful wife, Veronica, have four ridiculously cute kids: Kharis, Alethia, Ryah, and Adon. Unless God calls him elsewhere, J. D. plans to stay at the Summit Church until he preaches his last sermon at his own funeral before saying goodbye and hopping into the casket.

Spence Shelton developed this Bible study. Spence is the lead lastor of Mercy Church in Charlotte, North Carolina. Mercy Church launched in September 2015 with the vision of seeing a gospel awakening move through the people of Charlotte and extend to the ends of the earth.

Spence has coauthored several books, including *The People of God* and the small-group studies *Jesus the King, The Meaning of Marriage, The Gospel according to Jonah,* and *Presence: Overwhelmed by God*.

Spence earned a BS in business administration from the University of North Carolina in Chapel Hill and an MDiv in Christian ethics from Southeastern Baptist Theological Seminary. Spence and his wife, Courtney, have four children: Zeke, Ben, Ellie, and Haddie.

Welcome to a Gospel Revolution!

For many years my Christianity seemed to consist of a list of things to do and not to do. The results were spiritual frustration and weariness. Learning to dwell on the gospel changed all that. It produced in me the one thing religion couldn't: a *desire* for God.

The gospel isn't just the way we begin in Christ; it's also the way we grow in Christ. Dwelling on the gospel produces freedom, joy, radical sacrifice, and audacious faith. The gospel has revolutionized my life, and it has revolutionized our church. I believe it will revolutionize yours too.

In light of that conviction, I'd like to encourage you to do a couple of things concurrently with this Bible study. For the next eight weeks, pray the four parts of the gospel prayer and read along with me the four Gospels: Matthew, Mark, Luke, and John.

Why? Because I want you to saturate yourself in the gospel every day. The most gospel-centered books ever written are the Gospels. You'll find Jesus there. Dwell with Him in the Gospels for eight weeks and let the gospel prayer saturate your heart and mind with His beauty and love. I think you'll never be the same.

Here's the gospel prayer that we'll learn more about in the weeks ahead.
Part 1: "In Christ there's nothing I can do that would make You love me more, and there's nothing I've done that would make You love me less."
Part 2: "Your presence and approval are all I need for everlasting joy."
Part 3: "As You've been to me, so I'll be to others."
Part 4: "As I pray, I'll measure Your compassion by the cross and Your power by the resurrection."

Blessings to you as you begin your gospel revolution!

J. D. Greear

Gospel Reading Plan

Begin the following forty-day Gospel reading plan after your first small-group session. To stay on track, read and check off five passages each week.

	DAY	READING			DAY	READING	
☐	1	Matthew 1–2	Week 1	☐	21	Luke 5–6	Week 5
☐	2	Matthew 3–4		☐	22	Luke 7	
☐	3	Matthew 5–7		☐	23	Luke 8–9	
☐	4	Matthew 8–9		☐	24	Luke 10–11	
☐	5	Matthew 10–12		☐	25	Luke 12–13	
☐	6	Matthew 13–14	Week 2	☐	26	Luke 14–16	Week 6
☐	7	Matthew 15–16		☐	27	Luke 17–19	
☐	8	Matthew 17–18		☐	28	Luke 20–21	
☐	9	Matthew 19–20		☐	29	Luke 22–24	
☐	10	Matthew 21–23		☐	30	John 1–2	
☐	11	Matthew 24–25	Week 3	☐	31	John 3–4	Week 7
☐	12	Matthew 26–28		☐	32	John 5–6	
☐	13	Mark 1–3		☐	33	John 7–8	
☐	14	Mark 4–5		☐	34	John 9–10	
☐	15	Mark 6–7		☐	35	John 11–12	
☐	16	Mark 8–10	Week 4	☐	36	John 13–14	Week 8
☐	17	Mark 11–13		☐	37	John 15–16	
☐	18	Mark 14–16		☐	38	John 17	
☐	19	Luke 1–2		☐	39	John 18–19	
☐	20	Luke 3–4		☐	40	John 20–21	

The *Gospel* Experience

Welcome to an eight-week journey through the Gospels that we hope will lead you, as well as your church, to a gospel revolution. Here's how the study works.

Introduction. Each week begins with a narrative overview of the weekly topic. You'll probably want to read this introduction before your group meets so that you'll better understand the topic and the context for the group session.

Start. Your actual group session will most likely begin here with an icebreaker that's designed to help you ease into the study and get everyone talking. A brief description of J. D.'s teaching helps set the stage for hearing from God during each video teaching segment.

Watch. Key statements from the video session are provided so that you can follow along and take notes as J. D. teaches.

Discuss. These questions help the group study passages that reinforce J. D.'s teaching in the video. Each question is designed to lead the group deeper into the gospel so that the gospel becomes foundational in members' lives. These questions facilitate the work that the Holy Spirit is accomplishing in the lives of individuals and the group.

Respond. These gospel exercises allow group members to enjoy a smaller group experience, which increases the likelihood that everyone's voice will be heard. Although some of these activities introduce further opportunities for Bible study, some focus on prayer, meditation, and encouragement.

Close. This section concludes the group session and summarizes key points. It also offers a final challenge and a time to pray together.

Personal study. Three or four devotions are provided each week to be completed after the group session. These devotions complement the Gospel reading plan so that group members are immersed in the pool of the gospel throughout this *Gospel* experience.

Week I
GOSPEL CHANGE

God doesn't *need* anything from us.

Hear this plainly. God doesn't *need* anything from us. What God *wants* is the affections of our heart.

Our opening week's study explores the core concepts of living a gospel-centered life. Many Christians are living in a difficult tension. They're fighting to follow the teachings of Jesus and the commands of Scripture, yet the result isn't the abundant life they long for. They may be bringing their behavior in line with God's rules, but their hearts are still running from Him. Usually without realizing it, they've let God their Father take a back seat to God their Judge. As a result, they're left in a daily grind trying to appease God. The end of this road is either empty religious routine or abandonment of the Christian faith altogether. Both are a far cry from the revolutionary power of the gospel that Jesus unleashed on earth.

The primary aim of this first week's study will be to develop a clear distinction between religious change and gospel change. The common theme in the Scriptures and in this week's study is that God doesn't want more religious conformity; He wants our love. We have a tendency in religious circles to fill our lives to the brim with religious activities. For the most part, these activities in themselves are good, God-honoring pursuits. The reality, however, is that habitual Christianity may be the number-one killer of the joy-filled life Christ has offered us. A good question for us is, Are we trying to earn God's love and affection, or are we living in the joy of God's love that's been declared over us in the gospel?

>>> Start

If you grew up in church, what do you remember most about it? If you didn't, what was your impression, if any, of church?

Do you recall anything about your past church experience that now seems antiquated, funny, or out of place?

Begin this week by answering a few questions below. Ask everyone to record their answers. We'll return to these questions in group session 8 to observe ways we've changed. Think of this activity like preparation for a workout or a diet. Though it's painful, good wisdom says to get on the scale and see where you are so that later you can celebrate how much you've changed. In this case, however, we'll celebrate how much *God* has changed us!

In your own words, what's the gospel?

Why did you become a Christian, or why would you want to?

What do you hope to gain from this study during the next eight weeks?

When you hear the word *gospel,* what comes to mind? Many of us have some exposure to this word, whether from church, media, or pop culture. But do any of us really grasp the significance that the gospel could have on our everyday lives? Do we understand the power available to us in the gospel? In video session 1 J. D. Greear introduces the concept of a gospel-centered life and its power to unlock the power and joy we may be missing.

Watch

Watch video session 1.

Mechanical change is change from the outside. That is how you change things that aren't alive.

Religion changes you externally by adding things to your life.

In organic change, your behavior changes because you change.

You worship whatever you deem essential for life and happiness.

What God desires is a heart that desires Him.

The gospel tells you not to change in order to earn the approval of God but because you have the approval of God.

The gospel reveals God's beauty in a way that we begin to desire Him.

The gospel reveals God's mercy so that we begin to love Him.

Gospel-centered change is not about giving you a list of things you need to go and do for God but making you stand in awe of what He has done for you.

Video sessions available at lifeway.com/gospel
or with a subscription to smallgroup.com

⋙ Discuss

Use the following questions to discuss the video teaching.

How would you summarize the key message of this session's video teaching? Did anything surprise you or challenge you in a way you didn't expect?

Read 1 Corinthians 15:1-4. Based on these verses, what's the gospel? Work together to arrive at a scriptural definition for the group moving forward.

The gospel, in its essence, is the message that Jesus lived a perfect life, died a sacrificial death, was buried, and rose on the third day in victory over sin and death. The whole Bible centers on this revelation.

Let's start looking at what the apostle Paul had to say about the gospel.

Read Paul's prayer in Ephesians 3:16-21. What requests did Paul make on the people's behalf?

What does the nature of Paul's requests tell you about what he believed to be central to the Christian life? How might his beliefs differ from what we often believe to be the primary purpose of the Christian life?

Paul tells us that God initiates and grants us the ability to know and love Him. Hearing the gospel informs us, but the Holy Spirit transforms us. How does this understanding affect the way we approach life change?

The love of God for us is an abundant well we draw from to live our lives for His glory. Jesus Christ taught and embodied this love.

> **Read Matthew 22:37-39. Here Christ quoted Deuteronomy 6:4-9, which was a central prayer for the Jewish community. Why do you think Christ called this the greatest commandment? How did Jesus expand the commandment given in Deuteronomy?**

> **Read Luke 7:44-48. Jesus affirmed the faith of a sinful woman by showing how much she loved God because of how much she'd been forgiven. What obstacles keep us from having faith like this woman on a daily basis?**

The love of Christ, most visibly displayed in the gospel, is more valuable than anything else. Now we'll investigate ways His love plays out in daily life.

> **Which statement tends to be truer of the way you operate on a daily basis—"I love because He first loved me" or "I love because I'm supposed to"? What's the difference between these two ideas?**

> **Although the Christian life is supposed to be freeing, many times we feel burdened by it. What do you find to be the most difficult part of being a Christian? What are some possible reasons? How does the gospel bring a fresh perspective?**

Respond

Divide into same-gender groups of two or three people. As each group discusses the prompts below, everyone should write down his or her answer. After ten minutes reconvene as a group.

In three words describe what the gospel means to you personally.

Discuss with your smaller groups why you chose those three words. When you reconvene with the rest of the group, a couple of people should share their responses.

Close

The center of the Christian faith isn't a set of rules to follow but a loving Father who rescues His children from death and gives them new life. Once we start to realize His love for us, the natural response is to love Him in return. Love for God is the core of Christianity. In this love we joyfully live in step with the design for living that He has given us in the Scriptures. We aren't under the rule of an exacting dictator who demands that we earn His favor but under the care of a Father whose instructions flow from His love for us.

Pray together.

This Week
MATTHEW 1–12

This week's personal study begins our intense, eight-week spiritual workout of reading all four Gospels. This week's Gospel reading is Matthew 1–12. Refer to the reading plan below to find out what passages to read each day.

On the following pages you'll find three devotional thoughts designed for you to use in conjunction with your daily Gospel readings.

This Week's Reading Plan

Day 1 ❯ Matthew 1–2

Day 2 ❯ Matthew 3–4

Day 3 ❯ Matthew 5–7

Day 4 ❯ Matthew 8–9

Day 5 ❯ Matthew 10–12

THE FAMILY TREE

The opening chapter of the Gospel of Matthew begins with a look at Jesus' family tree. Verse 1, "An account of the genealogy of Jesus Christ, the Son of David, the Son of Abraham," wouldn't have been lost on the first-century Jewish audience to which Matthew's Gospel account was tailored. David and Abraham were two of the most prominent figures in Jewish history, and God gave both men a covenant promising that the Savior of the world would come through their lineage. Although the announcement in this verse may appear to us to be nothing more than opening movie credits, we'd be better served to see this genealogy as credentials—proof that Jesus is who He said He was in Matthew's Gospel. These verses establish Jesus' royal right to the throne of God's people.

Now that the significance of Jesus' lineage is clear, notice the makeup of the people listed in the first sixteen verses. It wouldn't be uncommon in that day to establish someone's lineage through a genealogy like this. What's uncommon is acknowledging women in such a list. This honor was normally reserved for men because they were the heads of households. How astonished readers must have been to see King David's name in the same sentence as Rahab's and Ruth's! Five women in all, two Gentiles and three of questionable character, are included in the genealogy of the Messiah. Heroes, kings, Gentiles, prostitutes, adulterers—Matthew was being very intentional with his list.

We then cut right to the announcement and brief birth scene of Jesus Christ. The miraculous is introduced just eighteen verses into our reading. Think about it. An angel came to tell a virgin woman that she would be with child from the Holy Spirit. The child's name meant "God is with us" (v. 23), and He would save us from our sins. The supernatural hand of God was all over this setting. What a scene! It feels unbelievable, but should we expect any less from God Himself? We're only in chapter 1, but Jesus has arrived, and as you may expect, it's kind of a big deal.

REFLECT

What does the inclusion of women and Gentiles alongside kings and heroes in Jesus' lineage foreshadow about the kingdom that Jesus was inaugurating? How have you personally benefited from that kingdom?

Look at the angel's announcement in verse 21. What was to be Jesus' primary purpose? What does that purpose mean to you?

PRAY & MEDITATE

Pray that God will allow this one purpose of Jesus to rest in your mind and that it would declutter the various notions of Jesus that swirl in our culture. In a gospel-centered mind Jesus is first and foremost our Savior and Lord.

Day 2 Matthew 4

LOVE CONQUERS ALL

Jesus had just heard the words of His Father: "This is my beloved Son, with whom I am well-pleased" (3:17). This is what every son longs to hear from his father. Immediately after His baptism, Christ was led out to be tempted by the Devil (see 4:1). What was Christ's motivation for resisting Satan? It was the words of His Father. Because His Father love Him so much, the temptations of Satan lost their luster, and Jesus revealed them for the frauds they were. The best way you and I can fight temptation is by resting deeper in Christ's love for us. When we have all of our needs met in His love, temptation no longer has a hold over us.

A friend of mine gave me an idea I've begun to use with my kids to help get this concept across. Every so often I look at my children and tell them I love them. Not too revolutionary, I know. But I follow that with the question "Why does Daddy love you?" They're still young, so their answers vary from "I don't know" to "I love Daddy" to "Pretzels!" After a moment or two I tell them the answer: "Because you're my children!"

Only a couple of months into this practice, they're already beginning to catch on. I want them to know as they grow up that their father's love isn't based on a merit system but on their identity. As they grow up, opportunities to question that love will come from every angle. Whether they reject me by lying to me or disobeying me or sense rejection from me because they feel they've let me down, Satan will use such seasons to cause my children to run from me. In those moments I want them to hear something familiar from me: "Why does Daddy love you? Because you're my children." I don't love them because they deserve it but because of who they are. I want that understanding to drive them back into my arms, not farther from me.

This is God's call to us. In Christ we're God's children, and we can rest in His unwavering love for us.

REFLECT

Satan began his attack on Jesus by questioning the very identity that God had just spoken over Jesus: *"If you are the son of God ..."* (Matt. 4:3, emphasis added). Satan does the same to us. How can you remember your identity as God's child this week?

In what ways are you currently being tempted? How does the truth that God is pleased with you (because of Christ) help you in that struggle? Or if you have a hard time believing God is pleased with you, what truth in today's Scripture can you depend on?

God calls us to carry one another's burdens (see Gal. 6:2) and to promote love and good works (see Heb. 10:24). Who's another believer you could practice those ministries with on a consistent basis? Try to take those actions this week.

PRAY & MEDITATE

Romans 8:1-2 says:

> *There is now no condemnation for those in Christ Jesus,*
> *because the law of the Spirit of life in Christ Jesus*
> *has set you free from the law of sin and death.*

Will you take time now to thank God that you're free from the power of sin over you? Ask Him to help you live today, especially in difficult moments, in a constant awareness of and satisfaction in that freedom.

Day 3 Matthew 6

WHY SHOULD WE PRAY?

This is the question the disciples asked Jesus. In truth, it's the question that keeps many people from developing rich prayer lives. Most people want to believe prayer works, but they have no idea where to start. So when the need to pray arises, they offer God a skeptical but desperate plea to fix what's broken in their lives. Often a lack of confidence in prayer turns into a mundane routine with little or no variance and little or no connection with God.

How did Jesus respond to this question? While the question that the disciples asked is recorded in Luke 11:1, the full response Christ gave is recorded in Matthew 6:5-13. We refer to this famous passage as the Lord's Prayer, though it would be far more accurate to call it the Disciples' Prayer since it's Jesus' prescription for our prayer lives. I hope a look at this passage will free you to begin praying with confidence in the way God designed prayer to be practiced. Here are some ways Jesus instructed us to pray.

- Pray to an audience of one (see vv. 5-6).

- The heart matters, not the tongue (see vv. 7-8).

- Prayer is first God-centered (see vv. 9-10).

- Pray as if your life depended on it (see vv. 11-13).

Of course, prayer flows from a heart captivated by the gospel.

REFLECT

Does your prayer life feel vibrant or mundane? Which of the four elements on the previous page is your weakest link? How will the gospel change your perspective?

I've recommended that you read the gospel prayer every week throughout this Bible study (see p. 5). How is the gospel prayer already challenging your prayer life? How does praying it affect the rest of your day?

PRAY & MEDITATE

There would be no better passage to meditate on today than Matthew 6:5-13. Pray the way Christ called His disciples to pray, but don't just recite the Lord's Prayer. The psalmist's prayer was:

> *May the words of my mouth*
> *and the meditation of my heart*
> *be acceptable to you,*
> *LORD, my rock and my Redeemer.*
> **PSALM 19:14**

Meditate on these words. Let them become your words from your mind and heart, not just words on a page. Then pray them to God.

Week 2
GOSPEL DISCOVERY

Is your heart captivated by the glory and
beauty of God? Are you overcome by a sense
of awe and drawn by a feeling of intimacy?

What we eat, wear, drive, read, and buy is almost always governed by how pleasing it is to our senses. If an eight-ounce filet mignon looks hot off the grill and smells of melted blue cheese crumbled on top, I'll eat the entire thing with a big grin. If, however, that same cut of meat is rotten and maggot-infested, I'm repulsed! What I see determines my desires. My desires then dictate my decisions.

In the same way, my spiritual senses, namely spiritual sight, inform my beliefs. The apostle Paul called this spiritual sight the eyes of the heart (see Eph. 1:18). What I sense to be most valuable, most beautiful, and most desirable is what I'll order my life to obtain and retain. Paul's prayer, which must become our prayer, is that we begin to see the riches and beauty of God, found most prominently in the gospel.

Start

What's the most breathtaking sight you've ever seen? What overwhelmed you about it?

Have you recently made any life-changing decisions? Without going into all of the details, what compelled you to make or stick with your decision?

Last week we began our study of the revolutionary power of the gospel. J. D. taught us the difference between religious behavior and gospel-centered change. We saw that Christ seeks our hearts, not our deeds. As our hearts change to desire Him more, our lives will change to follow Him more.

This week we'll press deeper into our discovery of the power of the gospel. We'll see in Exodus 19 that the Israelites were overwhelmed by the magnitude of God's size, holiness, and grace. What they saw changed them forever. In Christianity, change begins with sight.

How did your personal study of Matthew 1–12 go? What stood out most to you from your reading?

The gospel message isn't confined to just a few verses tucked away in the first four books of the New Testament. It's the rushing river of God's salvation story that runs straight through the heart of the entire Bible. From beginning to end, the love of God for His children is intended to motivate us to obey Him. In this session J. D. works through the Scriptures to build on last week's idea of gospel-motivated change. We'll explore the way realigning our hearts will realign our lives.

Watch

He gave them a glimpse of His unimaginable size.

He shows them His untouchable holiness.

He shows them His unfathomable grace.

What we most need is to see God.

Gospel change is being overwhelmed by the glory of God to the extent that it brings into captivity all your other passions.

Lesser affections are driven out by a greater passion for God, and that passion for God is created by learning of His passion for me.

Video sessions available at lifeway.com/gospel
or with a subscription to smallgroup.com

⟫⟫ Discuss

Use the following questions to discuss the video teaching.

> As J. D. taught these Scriptures, what passage captured your attention? Why?

> J. D. acknowledged that the gospel has rooted out sins in his life. Did that admission resonate with you? When have you seen a similar pattern in your own life?

Hopefully you noted that life change can come only from a completely renewed source of our desires and affections. Let's look at the way Jesus sustains us in that new life.

> Read Hebrews 12:1-2. The author used the language "keeping our eyes on Jesus" (v. 2), picturing Him as our focal point. Knowing we can't physically see Jesus, what do you think it looks like to keep our spiritual eyes on Jesus?

> What most often distracts you from Jesus? Why do you think it has so much strength and influence?

> How could you change this week's routine in order to keep your focus on Christ?

Now that we've looked at the way Christ sustains a gospel revolution in our lives, let's explore the way this work plays out on a daily basis.

Read Ephesians 5:1-2. We love because we've been loved. In what areas of your life is loving others most difficult right now? Discuss your setbacks in this area.

The answer to the previous question usually reveals where the gospel most needs to go to work in your life. How can the gospel help you overcome these challenges?

Read 2 Corinthians 4:16-18. Verse 16 says our renewal occurs "day by day." What do you think the gospel implications are for the way we live?

Respond

Divide into same-gender groups of two or three people. Each smaller group should respond to the prompts below. After ten minutes, reconvene and share responses.

Read Galatians 5:16-23 and answer the following questions.

When you read this passage as indicative (what it says about who you are) instead of imperative (what it tells you to do), how does your response change?

Circle the word *desire(s)* each time it appears in this passage. Why do you think this word is so significant in a believer's life?

Close

In this session we saw that the gospel story is told throughout the pages of Scripture. We understood that God's beauty and grace change us from the inside, resulting in change on the outside. Our study of the Scriptures revealed Jesus to be the ongoing focal point on whom we fix our eyes at all times, and we looked at tangible ways to experience that focus in the coming week. Ultimately, God doesn't force us to do anything. Rather, He shows us Himself in His love for us. His love changes our hearts and frees us to act on our new desires. Led by the Spirit, our lives bear the fruit of the Spirit.

Pray together.

This Week
MATTHEW 13-23

Week 2 of our eight-week study of the Gospels will be our last full week in the Gospel of Matthew. This week we'll encounter the epic saga of Jesus' life and ministry. Parables, miracles, healings, conspiracies, execution, and more are all wrapped up in just a few pages. Refer to the following reading plan to stay on track this week.

On the following pages you'll find devotional thoughts that are designed to use in conjunction with your Gospel readings. These commentaries will push you deeper into the gospel-centered life you're being challenged to live.

This Week's Reading Plan

Day 1 Matthew 13

WHAT'S HE TALKING ABOUT?

Parables are intended to teach one main principle or point. Today we'll focus on Matthew 13:1-23. Here Jesus taught a parable to a crowd and then explained it to His disciples. He didn't always explain His parables as He did here, so this passage provides great insight for us. In the well-known parable of the sower, Jesus talked about four different types of soil. He then acknowledged that the seed represents the gospel, and the different types of soil represent the different types of people who hear the gospel message.

The first person hears the gospel, but the evil one comes like a bird and snatches away what has been sown. The second excitedly hears the gospel, but because he doesn't allow it to take root, he returns to his former idols when he faces hardship. The third person hears and believes, but the gospel gets choked out by the cares of the world and the deceitfulness of riches. The fourth person has the gospel rooted deeply in his soul; as a result, he produces much fruit over his lifetime.

Jesus' point is that the evidence of a life transformed by the gospel will be revealed over a lifetime. Notice the three enemies of planting and growing the gospel in someone's life.

1. The first is Satan. Jesus was acknowledging a real enemy who pursues and attacks people who hear and respond to the gospel.
2. The second enemy of the gospel is the failure to count the cost of following Christ. When tribulation occurs "because of the word" (v. 21), this person falls away. Following Christ for a while is convenient in many cases. But when functional saviors come into conflict with the gospel, many people drop Jesus for something else they think will solve their problem.
3. The final enemy may be the most potent in the church. The "worries of this age" look like anxiety, and the "deceitfulness of wealth" (v. 22) sounds like the promise that money provides security and happiness.

These enemies circle believers, waiting to pounce. But they don't prevail against the those who yield themselves to the gospel and allow it to take root in their souls and wield authority in their lives.

REFLECT

Notice that all but the first soil initially respond positively to the gospel. In what way does this fact warn us about church practice in the present day?

In what areas of your life are you preventing the gospel from taking root—from penetrating places where you really don't want it to go? How does this passage encourage you to let the gospel take root and grow in you?

PRAY & MEDITATE

Consider your openness to the gospel. Pray that God will break you of any pride that would keep the gospel from taking root in your life. Ask Him to protect you from the enemy as you begin to follow Jesus in areas of your life that perhaps you've never surrendered to Him before. Pray that your life will bear fruit (or evidence) of the grace God has given you.

Day 2 Matthew 16

BEHIND ENEMY LINES

Today we'll look at Matthew 16:13-20. Here we find a text that becomes a deeper and deeper well of truth the more we explore it. Jesus posed a question to His disciples: "Who do people say that the Son of Man is?" (v. 13). The disciples were probably eager to answer this one; it was the easy small-group question of that day. Jesus wanted to talk about what culture was saying. Then Jesus redirected His question to the disciples: "Who do you say that I am?" (v. 15). Peter's response is critical to the account. In what's often called the great confession, he proclaimed Jesus to be the promised Messiah, the Christ, the Son of the living God. Jesus celebrated the spiritual sight God had given to Peter.

Then Jesus said something profound: the church would be founded on the confession Peter had made. It's the first time Jesus had said the word *church*. This is significant. The church would be built not on Peter but on the truth he proclaimed: that Jesus was who He said He was. And notice what Jesus went on to say: "The gates of Hades will not overpower it" (v. 18).

Gates aren't offensive weapons. They're defensive measures. They guard. But Jesus was saying the gospel confession has the power to penetrate the gates of hell and bring people from death into life. This is the mission of the church Jesus talked about in verse 19. We attack the gates of hell with the gospel and watch it pull people who were dead in their sin and bound for hell out of their hopelessness and into freedom. What a mission we have!

REFLECT

How does your perception of the gospel change when you think of it as an offensive weapon to be used against the enemy?

How does the reality that you're in spiritual wartime, not peacetime, affect your daily life? Why should it?

PRAY & MEDITATE

Whether or not you daily acknowledge it, you're in a war. While your enemy isn't merciful, he's not more powerful than the gospel either. Pray for God to keep the gospel ready in your heart and mind as you'd hold on to a weapon during a battle. Pray for the salvation of your friends and family who are on the other side of the gates of hell. Finally, ask God to mold your local church into the image of the guardian and carrier of the gospel that Christ talked about in Matthew 16.

Day 3 Matthew 18

RADICAL FORGIVENESS

Today we continue mining the depths of the gospel through a parable Jesus told His disciples about forgiveness, found in Matthew 18:23-35. In this parable a guy owes a wealthy king ten thousand talents (one talent equaled twenty years' wages) or, put another way, more money than you or I will probably ever make in a lifetime. So the guy, unable to pay the king, knows he's bound for prison or worse, so he begs for mercy and time to pay his debt. In a twist that would have shocked his listeners, Jesus said the king has compassion on this man and completely forgives his large debt. What astounding mercy!

With his huge burden forgiven, this guy walks outside and runs into a coworker who owes him a few dollars. The forgiven man demands his five bucks, and when the coworker can't produce it, he has this man thrown into prison!

At this point Jesus' listeners were probably thinking this was ridiculous. No way would a guy forgiven that much refused to forgive such a little debt. And that's exactly Jesus' point. You see, the gospel message is one of radical forgiveness. The more we come to understand who God is and who we are, the bigger God's forgiveness of our sins becomes in our eyes. If we have trouble forgiving others, this means we have a gospel problem! It means we haven't understood how much we've been forgiven. Forgiveness and its twin sister, generosity, flow from a constant awareness of the forgiveness we've experienced.

REFLECT

Do you hold grudges? Do you have a hard time forgiving wrongs? How can you preach the gospel to yourself in this area of your life?

Do you need to forgive anyone this week? List people who come to mind and forgive as you've been forgiven.

PRAY & MEDITATE

Forgiveness isn't easy, but it's foundational to the Christian life. Ask God to give you a fresh awareness of the forgiveness He's given you through Christ and pray that His mercies will be new to you today. Pray that He will humble you and grant you peace as you seek to forgive people in your life who've wronged you. For those you've wronged, ask God for humility and love to seek forgiveness and reconciliation. Pray that His Spirit will bring unity to that relationship.

Day 4 Matthew 22

THE GREAT COMMANDMENT

Scattered throughout Scripture are key passages that tie it all together. They're like columns that connect and provide the foundation for the entire counsel of Scripture. Matthew 22:34-40 is one of those texts. We briefly looked at it in group session 1, but today we'll explore it further.

In this scene the Pharisees attempted to trap Jesus in His teachings so that they could undermine His ministry. When asked what the greatest command in the law is, Jesus recited another pivotal text, Deuteronomy 6:4-5. Jesus said loving God is the greatest command. Do you see the paradox? Love can't be forced. It voluntarily aligning your affections with what you desire most. Yet this is the greatest command!

Christ was acknowledging that at the center of the Christian faith isn't a set of rules but a relationship between a Father and His children. When we begin to experience God's love for us, seen in the glory of the gospel, we respond with love for Him. Furthermore, not only do we love Him, but we also show that love by loving our neighbor. Love for our neighbor is the natural outworking of love for God.

REFLECT

As you consider the Great Commandment, make a list of the things you love about God—who He is and what He's done for you.

How can your love for God motivate you to love your neighbor?

With whom can you discuss loving God and others so that they can encourage you in the gospel this week?

PRAY & MEDITATE

Everything we do flows from our love for God. Yet trying to love Him just creates another to-do list. Instead, ask God to open your mind and heart to receive His love for you. Pray that He will awaken you to the Father-child relationship He wants to have with you. Also ask God for wisdom and insight into relationships with your neighbors and for the ability to love them as you've been loved.

Week 3
GOSPEL ACCEPTANCE

In Christ there's nothing I can do that would
make You love me more, and there's nothing
I've done that would make You love me less.

The Gospel Prayer, Part 1

The gospel affirms that God completely accepts us once for all in Christ. Christ took our place as sinners and died the death we deserved to die; in return, we get to take His place as sons and daughters, receiving all the rights and privileges that were due to Him. God couldn't love us any more than He does right now because He couldn't love Christ any more than He does right now, and we're in Christ.

At eight weeks old my son had a fever so high that we had to take him to the emergency room. We were nervous. Worst-case scenarios began rolling through my head as I drove my wife and child to the hospital. Do you know what the worst part was for me? I could do nothing to cure my son. Nothing. Everything in me wanted to fix the problem. I wanted control, and I hated not having it.

The same is true of the way we often come to God. We think if we can manipulate the way we come to God, we can control the way He responds to us. We desperately want control of the one thing God was wise enough to leave us powerless over: His love for us. The gospel declares love over us precisely in our helplessness. This week we'll explore together what living in God's amazing grace is all about.

⟫⟫ Start

Have you ever had to cover for somebody? If possible, describe a time when you had to take the rap for someone else. How did things work out?

What's the best gift you've ever received or inherited? Why?

Last week J. D. taught us about the size, holiness, and love of God that Israel experienced in Exodus 19. We saw that the exposure to who God really is generated a life of obedience in Israel. Paul prayed a similar prayer in Ephesians 3:14-19: that first and foremost we'd know the love of God. Paul knew that true, lasting change comes from knowing more of who God is by experiencing Him.

How did your personal study of Matthew 13–23 go? What did God reveal to you?

Over the past week has any area of your life been particularly affected by what you're learning in *Gospel?* If so, explain.

In this session we'll begin to unpack the gospel prayer we've been praying together for the past two weeks. Underscoring this prayer is an important premise: when God looks at us, He sees Christ. J. D. will take us through his own journey in the gospel prayer, showing that living in the freedom of the gospel is counterintuitive to the way we've been conditioned to live. We'll look at methods the enemy uses to trap us in our religious tendencies, and we'll build on a strong foundation for the rest of our study of *Gospel*.

Watch

Watch video session 3.

Religion focuses on external changes. The gospel focuses on the heart.

With religion, we obey to get something from God. The gospel changes us so that we obey because we love God.

With religion, we change to earn the approval of God. In the gospel, we change because we have the approval of God.

There is nothing I can do that would make You love me more and nothing I have done that makes You love me less.

The gospel says you are accepted; therefore, obey.

Satan starts with what you did and tears down who you are. Jesus starts with who He's made you to be and then helps you rebuild what you did.

Those people who bear the most spiritual fruit are those who know that God's love for them is not dependent on their bearing of spiritual fruit.

Video sessions available at lifeway.com/gospel
or with a subscription to smallgroup.com

»»» Discuss

In what ways has the enemy attacked your identity in the past? How do those attacks affect the way you view sin in your life?

Read Matthew 4:1-11. Twice Satan said, "If you are the Son of God ..." (vv. 3,6). Why do you think Satan attacked Jesus' identity in this way? What might he have hoped to achieve?

Notice the way Christ responded to Satan's temptations. How does Christ's response serve as a model for us in responding to our temptations?

John 8:8-11 describes the way Christ looks at each of us. He declares us free from condemnation; then He commands us to live in that freedom. Why do you think it's so hard for us to follow Christ's command? How can we possibly make freedom confusing?

Read Ephesians 2:6-9. What do you think it means for us to be seated in the heavens now? How could this reality affect our view of works for God?

We've seen that our identity propels us to live free of Satan's attacks and condemnation. Let's turn our focus to what this freedom looks like in everyday life.

According to 2 Corinthians 5:17-21, God has made us new creations, as well as ministers of reconciliation and ambassadors for Him. How does this identity affect the way we live out our faith?

Read again part 1 of the gospel prayer: "In Christ there's nothing I can do that would make You love me more, and there's nothing I've done that would make You love me less." How can we incorporate this message into our role as ambassadors for Christ?

Now that we have action steps for the principles in this session, let's look once more into the identity Christ has given us.

Read Philippians 2:4-8. What does this passage tell us about Jesus' identity? In what ways does His confidence in His identity create a model for us? How should we then respond?

Respond

Divide into same-gender groups of two or three people and respond to the following questions. After ten minutes, reconvene and share your responses.

> **Read Colossians 3:1-4.**

Paul reminds us that just as Christ died, we've died. Our life is now hidden with Christ. This is the point of part 1 of the gospel prayer. God sees Christ, not us, when He looks at us. In verse 2 Paul gave us a new filter through which to look at our lives, so let's focus on that verse.

> **What does it look like for your mind to be on what's above when you're actually living in the rhythms of your life here on earth?**

> **Whom do you know who has modeled that focus for you? Share with the group some ways that person has influenced you.**

 # Close

In this session we've examined part 1 of the gospel prayer. We've seen ways the gospel combats our tendencies toward self-righteousness. We looked at ways God's acceptance of us through Christ initiates a love for God in us that religion simply can't create. Through Christ's confrontation with Satan in the wilderness, we identified one of Satan's primary means of attacking believers. He questions our standing with God—our identity—and then tries to tear us down. In contrast, God begins by assuring believers of their identity as His children.

> The Gospel Prayer, Part 1
>
> In Christ there's nothing I can do that would make You love me more, and there's nothing I've done that would make You love me less.

Pray together.

This Week
MATTHEW 24– MARK 7

This week we come to the dramatic end of Matthew's account of the life of Christ. The final five chapters of Matthew are our first encounter with Jesus' death, burial, and resurrection, commonly referred to as Christ's passion.

But it's not over when Matthew ends. More than any other Gospel writer, Mark gets right down to business. Before chapter 1 ends, you'll be knee-deep in Mark's account of the ministry of Jesus.

Refer to the following reading plan to stay on track this week. On the following pages you'll find devotional thoughts to use in conjunction with your Gospel readings. They not only provide commentary but also push you deeper into the gospel-centered life you're being challenged to live.

This Week's Reading Plan

WHAT'S SHE DOING?

In Matthew 26:6 Jesus was sitting down to dinner at Simon the leper's house. Wait. Jesus was at a leper's house? Most believe Jesus had healed Simon of his leprosy sometime before this meal, because lepers lived away from the general population. Simon's presence that night meant he had been healed. He had experienced firsthand the power of Jesus!

Keep reading; it gets better. The woman who approached Jesus in verse 7 was Mary, the sister of Martha and Lazarus—the same Lazarus whom Christ had resurrected from death. So Mary also had a firsthand knowledge of Jesus' power. She wasn't approaching a stranger; she was approaching her Savior. She became a perfect example of faith in a teachable moment between Christ and His disciples.

The occasion for this teachable moment occurred when Mary poured a very expensive flask of ointment on Jesus' head. Scholars say this ointment was worth about a year's wages. Did you get that? One year's wages. No wonder the disciples reacted the way they did (see vv. 8-9). Most churches and ministries work on nonprofit, slim-margin budgets, squeezing every penny as much as possible. How could this woman waste such valuable resources in such a seemingly unfit manner? That money could have been used for ministry!

Jesus' response to the disciples in this moment was crucial. He reminded them of the big picture (see vv. 10-12). What Mary recognized and what the disciples forgot was that the Messiah was right there in their midst! Everything else was secondary. The poor would always be there, but Jesus, the living God, was there for only a short time.

In this moment the disciples revealed their works righteousness. They believed they'd make a better impression on Christ by showing how much holier they would have been in using such a resource. Christ reminded the disciples that He was worth everything this woman owned. It was right for her to give everything she had to Him. He was the Son of God and their Savior!

REFLECT

Mary readily offered her most valued possession in worshiping Christ because He was more valuable than anything else to her. What's competing for your worship of Jesus? What would you have a difficult time sacrificing?

The disciples thought they were saying the right thing. But their desire to be holy got in the way of their love for Jesus. How are you structuring your life so that you remember to give Jesus your heart every day?

PRAY & MEDITATE

It's easy for us to lose the value of Christ in the immediate, everyday needs of life and even in the ministry needs of our local churches. Ask God to keep Jesus at the center of what you value and focus on and to help you identify what you value more than Him. Confess and repent of your idolatry. Also praise God because although you may lose sight of Christ sometimes, He never loses sight of you, nor does He value you less than He did when He died for you on the cross.

Day 2 Matthew 28

THE GREATEST MOMENT IN HUMAN HISTORY

Matthew 28 is so filled with meaning and implications for the Christian life. Preceding the events of this chapter was the crucifixion of Jesus in Matthew 27. The God-man was hanging dead on a cross. He was then buried in a tomb, and guards were stationed in front to ensure that no one stole His body. Though He said He was going to rise again, His disciples were huddled together, battling fear and uncertainty. But then, after three days Jesus of Nazareth got up and walked out of that tomb. The resurrection changed everything. This is why Paul said of the resurrection, "If we have put our hope in Christ for this life only, we should be pitied more than anyone" (1 Cor. 15:19).

The entire hope of the Christian life springs from the fact that the death of Christ for our sins was validated by His resurrection. The gospel tells us that sin and death were defeated once and for all when Christ walked out of the tomb. This changed everything. Christians now have hope because death is defeated. We have no fear in this world. We'll suffer, but we can suffer with hope. We'll face loss and grief, but we won't grieve as people who have no hope. These realities compelled Paul to say that he had "learned the secret of being content—whether well fed or hungry, whether in abundance or in need" (Phil. 4:12). The resurrection gives us a peace-filled confidence for whatever we encounter in this life.

Matthew didn't end with the resurrection. Chapter 28 ends with the famously titled Great Commission in verses 19-20. In this text Jesus compelled the disciples to make disciples as they were going through life. Notice that the imperative is "make disciples," not "go." Often this text is preached with an emphasis on missions. However, this isn't just a missions text; it's also a discipleship text. Are we living as disciples of Jesus? Is the gospel creating in us visible signs that we're His followers, not just fans? This passage tells us that part of such a life involves making other disciples. This is where the author leaves us—with Christ declaring His authority over the earth and giving the disciples the mission to make more disciples. Discipleship and missions go hand in hand.

REFLECT

Do you treat the Great Commission more like a command or a suggestion? Why?

Where in your life do you find the most joy in following Christ?

In what parts of your life do you most often ignore Christ's commands? What do you think causes you to do so?

PRAY & MEDITATE

If the resurrection weren't true, Christians would be most pitied. Thank God that Jesus got up out of the grave. Praise Him for this victory over sin and death. Thank God that He gives you new life just as He gave Jesus new life (see Rom. 6:4). The Great Commission calls us to make disciples, which begins by telling them this great news. Ask God to give you a new drive for making disciples and a clear idea of whom you could share the gospel with.

Day 3 Mark 2

GET UP!

If you're following the reading plan, you're reading the first seven chapters of the Gospel of Mark in the second half of this week. These passages are filled with occasions when Jesus asserted His authority over the earth, as we read about at the end of Matthew. Jesus cast out demons, healed the lame, and made nature obey His commands. He was giving the world signs of the kingdom of God. None of these signs were random; they had a purpose. Jesus was reversing the effects of sin in the world. Ultimately, His atoning death and resurrection would defeat the curse of sin and death once and for all!

This theme is clearly shown in Mark 2:1-12. A group of men brought a paralytic to Jesus in hopes that He would heal him. Word had already spread of Jesus' ability and willingness to heal people, and a crowd had packed the house in which He was staying. This paralytic man came looking for what he most wanted: physical healing. His life had been defined by his condition, and here was a glimmer of hope that things could finally change. In response to the man's faith and the faith of his friends, Jesus said, "Son, your sins are forgiven" (v. 5).

Is forgiving the man's sins what you expected Jesus to do? The man had an obvious physical need, and he was looking for physical, not spiritual, healing. Jesus met him that day in a way he wasn't expecting. The religious people in the crowd weren't ready for His response either. Jesus knew they were questioning His authority to forgive sins (see v. 7), and their skepticism opened the door for Jesus to make them understand the point of His ministry. Physical healing wasn't the point; it was simply a sign pointing to the soul healing Jesus would grant this man. But to prove He could forgive sins, Jesus commanded this guy to get up and walk. He did, and he was truly healed!

We often do the same thing this paralytic man did. We come to Jesus asking Him to give us what we want rather than what we need. It isn't wrong to pray and ask God for things. In fact, Jesus affirmed such an act of faith in this encounter. Jesus' point was that what you need most is His forgiveness.

REFLECT

What things are you asking God for right now?

The paralytic and his friends are examples of great faith. Do you truly believe God can do what you're asking of Him? Do you have a few friends who'll believe it with you? List their names here and ask them to pray with you in the days ahead.

If God said no, would you be OK with that answer? How do you respond when God declines your requests? How does your typical response need to change?

PRAY & MEDITATE

As you pray, read Philippians 4:4-7. Tell God that as much as you know how, you believe in His power and ability to provide what you're requesting of Him. Ask Him to give you a sense of peace about this matter by making Jesus' love for you bigger than what's going on in your life now and what will happen in the future. In this mindset, with thanksgiving, ask God to provide for you. Thank Him for all the ways He's provided for you in Christ.

Week 4
GOSPEL APPROVAL

Your presence and approval
are all I need for everlasting joy.
The Gospel Prayer, Part 2

Sometimes we act like adulterers. That's a disturbing analogy. What does it mean? As you know, an adulterer is someone who finds in someone else an intimacy he should find in his spouse. We're adulterers to God when we look for happiness, contentment, and security in places and people other than Him, the only true source of all those blessings.

When the founding fathers of the United States of America decided to fight for their freedom from British sovereignty, they laid out the case for their revolution in the well-known document called the Declaration of Independence. In the preamble, the most famous section of the document, they articulated the ideals behind their declaration. Perhaps no line is more repeated or well known than:

> We hold these truths to be self-evident, that all men are created equal, that they are endowed by their Creator with certain unalienable Rights, that among these are Life, Liberty and the pursuit of Happiness.[1]

That last right, the pursuit of happiness, has become a mantra almost synonymous with "the American way."

Thank God for a country that gives us such freedom. But we're adulterers when we use that freedom to seek other things more than God. Many of us search for joy on various unfulfilling paths, often forgetting to ask how to find fulfillment from the very one who created that desire within us. In this session we'll explore God's will for us and come to the conclusion that what or whom we're searching for has really been with us all along.

1. The Declaration of Independence, UShistory.org, accessed March 31, 2018, http://www.ushistory.org/declaration/document/.

»» Start

What extracurricular activity (not work or class) takes up the biggest portion of your free time? How does it contribute to or detract from your life?

If money weren't a problem and your job would be available when you got back, where would you go and what would you do for one year if you had the opportunity?

Last week we explored part 1 of the gospel prayer, which confronts self-righteousness. We saw that in the gospel God can't love us any more or any less than He does right now. Because Christians are hidden in Christ, when God looks at us, He sees only Christ and His righteousness. We learned that Satan's strategy to tear us down is to make us doubt the gospel identity God has given us. When we face guilt, fear, or doubt, we remember that God's love for us isn't based on anything we do. Christ's obedience to God on the cross became the source of our power to follow Him with our lives.

Did God use the teaching from last week to help you deal with a specific situation or life issue? If so, explain.

What major themes stood out to you in Matthew? What did you embrace about Jesus that you'd passed over before?

In session 4 we'll study part 2 of the gospel prayer to understand how the gospel confronts our idolatry. J. D. will teach us how to recognize the idols around which we're orienting our lives. The good news is that regardless of the depth of our idolatry, when we see Jesus for who He really is, we realize that He's better than any idols we've put in His place.

⟩⟩⟩ Watch

Watch video session 4.

Your presence and Your approval are all I need today for everlasting joy.

An idol is what we bow down to and serve.

An idol is whatever takes the place of God in your life, whatever you give "Godlike" weight to.

God is to have such weight in our lives that His presence and approval are all we need for everlasting joy.

Our ability to have joy in all things is the measure of how much we understand and believe the gospel.

Video sessions available at lifeway.com/gospel
or with a subscription to smallgroup.com

⟫⟫ Discuss

Use the following questions to discuss the video teaching.

How have you experienced Jesus as better and more fulfilling than the idols you've put in His place? Can you give a specific example?

Read Exodus 20:1-6, which J. D. referred to in the video. This famous passage begins the Ten Commandments, the foundational laws by which God intended Israel to function. What can you discern about the character of God in these verses?

Why do you think the Ten Commandments begin with a warning about idolatry? What does this priority reveal to you about what God knows about humanity?

Deuteronomy 6:4-5 is a key passage in the Old Testament. The Jewish community regularly recited it and still does today. How does it compare to Jesus' words in Matthew 22:37-40?

In these well-known Old Testament passages God warned Israel about idolatry, which would separate them from Himself. Sadly, we all sometimes fall victim to idolatry. Let's look at the way God responds to us when we run from Him.

Read Hosea 3:1. God equates idolatry with adultery. But how can this verse give you hope?

Read Ephesians 2:4-5, in which Paul reflected on the gospel. Our trespasses (see v. 5) are decisions to choose our ways over God's ways. What's the difference between being alive and being dead in these verses?

Because God is both just and merciful, He made a way to restore us even when we're in love with idols. Let's look at how we can live in light of this truth.

Philippians 4:4 calls for a life of rejoicing, and that's just the kind of life we long for. Joy is found in worshiping God. What does worship look like in your life? How do you rejoice in the Lord even during the most monotonous or painful seasons of your life? Give an example.

Do you have joy? Think of the five people you spend the most time with (friends, coworkers, spouse, kids, etc). On a scale of 1 to 10, with 1 being lowest and 10 being highest, how do you think each person would rate your level of joy? Why?

Respond

Divide into two groups: men and women. Don't worry; this isn't men versus women, and there will be no winner.

> **Read Romans 8:35-39 together. This a great passage about the permanence of God's love for us.**

> **What words represent threats to our relationship with God? What phrases cement our hope in the gospel?**

> **Discuss what this passage says about God's love for us.**

Whatever comes our way, no one and no thing is more powerful or precious than what God has given to us in the gospel. His love for us is closer to us than our own thoughts. The gospel teaches that in Christ we can never be separated from God.

Close

In this session we explored the reality that we're often tempted to look to things other than God to find happiness and security. We learned that these pursuits may give us temporary satisfaction but are ultimately empty in value because they can't give us the joy we're pursuing. In the idolatry test we looked at a series of questions to identify the idols in our lives. Most important, we fixed our eyes on Jesus and affirmed that His love and presence give us the permanent joy we were created to experience. The great fruit of the Christian life is that in Christ we can live each day with unshakable joy. This is the truth captured in part 2 of the gospel prayer. The presence and approval of Christ are all we need for everlasting joy. As we move into the second half of *Gospel,* we must do so with a spirit of humble joy found in the great mercy of God.

Pray together.

This Week
MARK 8–LUKE 4

This week you'll examine the rest of Mark's Gospel. With only sixteen chapters, Mark is the shortest of the four Gospels. Mark pointed his readers directly to Christ and focused on the plot highlights of Jesus' life. You'll encounter more miracles and more teachings, and again this week you'll read about the death, burial, and resurrection of Jesus. The beginning of Luke's Gospel has a very different feel than Mark's Gospel does. Notice the detail and order Luke tried to give his readers as the book begins.

What a great week in the Scriptures you have ahead of you! On the following pages you'll find devotional thoughts to use in conjunction with your Gospel readings. They'll provide commentary and push you deeper into the gospel-centered life you're being challenged to live.

This Week's Reading Plan

Day 16 ❯ Mark 8–10
Day 17 ❯ Mark 11–13
Day 18 ❯ Mark 14–16
Day 19 ❯ Luke 1–2
Day 20 ❯ Luke 3–4

Day I Mark IO

SELL IT ALL

In Mark 10:17-23 we encounter a young man who strongly desired to inherit the eternal life Jesus was teaching about. Though young, this man had great wealth and no doubt stature in his society because of it. For a man of his wealth to kneel before Jesus was certainly an act of humility. He knew of Jesus and wanted what Jesus was offering. When this man asked Jesus how he could obtain eternal life, Jesus began to look under the hood of this man's life. Interestingly, Jesus initially answered this question by reminding the rich young man of the Ten Commandments. Of course, Jesus knew that obeying these commandments couldn't earn salvation, but He was testing the man's heart.

The test came to a head in verses 21-22. Notice in verse 21 that Jesus loved the man. His command to sell everything and give it to the poor was stated in love. How do we know? Verse 22 reveals it. This man's wealth was his idol, so Jesus attacked it head-on. What looks like an attack on the man was actually an attack on the gates of hell. Jesus knew this man's wealth was evidence of an empty pursuit of happiness. In verse 23 Jesus acknowledged how difficult it is for people with wealth to love God and not money. And we can't love both.

We must recognize that the rich young man wasn't an evil businessman whose goal was to squeeze every dime he could out of everyone. He genuinely wanted to follow Jesus. He sought out Jesus and even showed some signs of submission to His authority. But Jesus didn't want some of this man's life; He wanted all of it. He knew this man's heart was ultimately tied to something other than God. His idolatry was clear when the man demonstrated by his departure that he was more comfortable with losing God than losing his wealth.

Idolatry is like a tiny thread woven throughout the fabric of our lives so intricately that we feel that pulling it out will kill us. Yet because God loves us so much, His gospel always confronts our idols head-on.

REFLECT

The rich young man gave wealth more significance than anything else in his life. What in your life are you likely to give more significance than God?

Jesus employed drastic measures to try and break the idol in this man's life. If you've identified your idols, what steps could you take to kick them off their pedestals? Talk to your spouse or a trusted friend when you're ready to take that step. They can encourage you on this gospel journey.

PRAY & MEDITATE

Greed and materialism have a way of weaving themselves so intricately into our lives that we don't realize how toxic they can become. Ask God to make you aware of what you value more than Christ and to build a willingness, even in the small things, to submit your agenda and desires to His agenda and desires. Thank Him for caring enough about your relationship with Him that He's willing to confront your idols head-on.

Day 2 Mark 13

BE READY

In the second half of the Book of Mark, we encounter multiple passages that address what will happen in the last days. The people surrounding Jesus, like everyone before and since, were trying to find out how everything in this world is going to end. While giving brief insights into the last days, Jesus gave a very important word on how His followers are to live until then, recorded in Mark 13:32-37. Jesus began this passage by acknowledging that no one, not even He, knows when the end will come. Only the Father knows. His words should free us from the influence of people who claim to know when the world will end.

The one thing Jesus tells us is to live ready—to be awake and keep on guard. He compared this world to the home of a man who went on a journey and left his servants in charge. The servants worked and kept the house prepared as if their master could return home at any moment. Jesus warned His followers to stay awake and ready.

How can we live in such a way that we remain ready for the end to come? It doesn't mean we don't make investments or long-term plans because we're waiting for Christ to return. On the contrary, we honor Christ by stewarding the resources He's given us. We can't cram for Christ's return; being ready is a way of life. This world and everything in it are God's; are you living as if this is true? People who are living for the next world and not this one are generous with their lives because they realize money holds no value in Christ's kingdom. They're kind to others because Christ has been kind to them. They live in joy because in the gospel they've found overwhelming joy for themselves. This is a ready life—one that seeks:

to act justly,
to love faithfulness,
and to walk humbly with your God.
MICAH 6:8

REFLECT

If Jesus returned right now, would you be ready? Why or why not?

In a world that's always trying to guess when the end will come, how do we as Christians find peace in Jesus' words and share it with others? How do we demonstrate that peace?

PRAY & MEDITATE

Christ's future return creates hope in Christians because it will usher in a world that will be free from the pain and brokenness of this world. Ask God to begin cultivating in your mind an active awareness of heaven so that you can live for things above and not things here on earth. Thank Him for the hope that comes with the promise of His return. Ask God to show you ways you can be more generous with your life and resources since, in light of heaven, treasures on earth have no eternal value.

Day 3 Mark 15

THE DEATH OF JESUS

Once a year many Christians celebrate Good Friday. The irony of the name, of course, is that it memorializes Jesus' death on the cross. So how can death, a consequence of sin, be good? Christ's death was good because on the cross God's wrath was satisfied. This is the beautiful news of the gospel. Our sin has left us at enmity with God. We've chosen our ways over God's ways, and the result is that we're bound for death. We need a Savior to restore us to our Father we've rebelled against. So Jesus gave His life in place of ours. We're now hidden with Christ.

Mark 15 records the crucifixion of Jesus. This horrific execution of the Son of God was for our benefit. That's the gospel in four words: Jesus in our place. At the crucifixion many people mocked and challenged Him to get down off the cross if He was really God, but Jesus stayed there in torment to complete His Father's plan for our salvation.

When Jesus breathed His last breath, the curtain of the temple was torn in two from top to bottom (see v. 38). This curtain had separated the dwelling place of God from the people of God. The literal curtain represented the figurative curtain: Jesus. As His body tore on the cross, He created a way for us to be with God. The curtain tore from the top because only God could create this means of salvation for us. We couldn't do it ourselves. No longer does God reside in temples made by humans. He resides in believers in the person of His Holy Spirit. We've been restored to the Father.

REFLECT

When you read Mark's account of Jesus' crucifixion, what stood out to you?

What emotions did you feel as you read about Jesus' death? Or have you heard the story so many times that you've lost sensitivity to its agony and power? If that's the case, ask God to help you grasp the extent of Jesus' suffering so that you can feel the weight of it and praise Him.

Articulate in your own words why the death of Jesus is so important to you.

PRAY & MEDITATE

At the cross we see God's love and justice come together in the death of Jesus. This moment changed everything. As you consider the cross, thank God for giving Jesus as a sacrifice to take your place and pay the penalty for your sin. Praise Him for forgiving you of your sin through the blood of Jesus and for restoring you to Himself. Finally, ask God for a sense of humility and joy that comes with remembering that nothing you could do—only what Jesus did—has given you new life.

Day 4 Luke 1

MARY'S SONG

The first two chapters of Luke are perhaps some of the most commonly read Scriptures among Christians, especially at Christmas. Luke 1:26-56 is our particular focus today. This passage is composed of both narrative (storytelling) and poetry. In verses 26-45 Luke narrated the angel's announcement of the birth of Christ to Mary, as well as Mary's visit to Elizabeth. Verses 46-55 are commonly called Mary's song. We shouldn't be surprised that it reads like a psalm. Mary had obviously committed many psalms to heart, and now God allowed her to be a conduit of His blessing.

Mary's song interrupts the flow of the narrative. Luke briefly paused from describing events so that his readers could understand what those events meant. The angel's announcement to Mary had extraordinary significance. Luke made clear that these events were rooted in the covenant promises God had made to the people of Israel. God had promised that a descendant of David would inherit his throne and permanently reign over Israel (see 2 Sam. 7:13,16; Isa. 9:6-7). Our key verse, Luke 1:31, confirms that Jesus fulfilled this promise.

In the opening chapters of this book, God used the least likely people in the least likely ways to finally bring the forever King into His kingdom. We encounter a young woman who believed the seemingly absurd, life-changing pronouncement made over her. Her belief was commended, and in a rare biblical aside, we're given a glimpse into her heart, where Mary, the mother of the King, treasured so many moments.

REFLECT

Try to put yourself in Mary's shoes. What would have been your own response to God?

Read Luke 1:37. This verse seems to explain the reason God chose a barren woman and a virgin as the mothers of John and Jesus: to display His power and majesty. How does this simple verse give you hope?

PRAY & MEDITATE

Mary received staggering news about the coming birth of Jesus, and her response rang of a servant's heart and mind. Ask God to give you a humble, joyful disposition like Mary's in response to His calling in your life for His glory. Remembering that nothing is impossible with God, ask Him for your needs. Thank God for His great redemptive plan, designed for you, that culminated in the life and death of Jesus.

Week 5
GOSPEL RESPONSE

As You've been to me, so I'll be to others.

The Gospel Prayer, Part 3

In October 2000 Warner Brothers released the movie *Pay It Forward*. The film chronicled the spread of the generosity-centered viral movement from its inception as an eleven-year-old boy's class project to its influence across the country. Assigned the task of finding a way to change the world for the better, the boy devised a charitable pyramid scheme in which the recipient of one favor, instead of simply returning the favor, did one favor each for three separate third parties. The film merited little acclaim, but the concept struck a familiar chord with many people. When we experience the benefit of someone's generosity toward us, it changes us. It calls for a response. Do we pay them back? Do we thank them and go on with life? Do we pay it forward? The one thing we feel we can't do, in good conscience, is to ignore the generosity of another person.

When we see the extraordinary generosity given to us in the gospel, we have no choice but to live a life of radical generosity in response. We forgive because we've been forgiven. We love because we've been loved.

Extravagant grace has propelled the church for the past two thousand years. Grace motivates more grace. Jesus taught this truth when He told His disciples to love one another as He had loved them (see John 13:34-35; 15:12,17). The New Testament reinforces this teaching throughout with statements like "If God loved us in this way, we also must love one another" (1 John 4:11). The Christian message is grace. The Christian life is simply grace motivating grace.

⟫⟫ Start

Have you ever done a random act of kindness for a complete stranger? What about for someone who wasn't a stranger? If so, describe the experience.

Can you recall a time when you extended grace by forgiving someone when it wasn't easy or fun to do? How did you feel? How did it affect your relationship?

Last week we examined part 2 of the gospel prayer: "Your presence and approval are all I need for everlasting joy." We saw that God created us to have joy. Although He intended for us to receive joy from Him, we often look for it in almost every other place. To have joy in all things depends on how much we understand and believe the gospel.

Learning to confront idols in our lives is a key step in spiritual growth. Did further reflection after last week's study make you aware of any idols in your life? Would you like to share any?

You've been praying the gospel prayer for four weeks now. How is God using that practice in your life as you seek to follow Him?

Did you read anything in Mark or the beginning of Luke that you hadn't noticed before or that surprised you? Explain.

This week J. D. will teach part 3 of the gospel prayer, which emphasizes living in radical response to the grace we've received in the gospel. We'll explore ways this radical grace should flow into every corner of our lives. Pay special attention to the way J. D. confronts guilt and greed-based motivations and replaces them with grace. This will be a critical foundation for moving into the second half of this Bible study.

Watch

As You have been to me, so I will be to others.

It's impossible to really believe the gospel and not also become like the gospel.

The generosity God has shown us in the gospel should change our attitude toward our stuff.

Those who are aware of God's mercy become merciful toward others.

Video sessions available at lifeway.com/gospel
or with a subscription to smallgroup.com

⟫⟫⟫ Discuss

Use the following questions to discuss the video teaching.

Which teaching point from the video had the greatest impact on you? Why?

J. D. said you're first a sinner; second, sinned against. What's your response to that teaching? Describe a situation in which you wish you had followed this principle.

In Exodus 36:2-7 Moses turned away the generous giving of Israel because it was so overwhelming. As you recall Israel's history of slavery in Egypt, what do you think compelled the people to engulf Moses with generosity?

If Christians have experienced even greater salvation than Israel, what do you think keeps us from living with joy-filled generosity today? How can Exodus 36:2-7 change your perspective?

Now that we've looked at Israel's response to God's provision, let's turn to the New Testament church to learn how we live in response to grace in light of the cross.

Read Acts 2:44-47. The early church pictured in the Book of Acts wasn't glamorous or perfect. But those messed-up sinners loved to take care of one another and regularly did so. How do you think caring for one another's needs can be a form of discipleship? What does this ministry look like in your life?

How could your group put the generosity of Christ on display in your community?

We've seen how the collective church responds to grace. Now let's look at ways the gospel creates a response in individual settings.

We all know people we feel have wronged us, and we want to get back at them. Paul addressed this situation in Romans 12:19-21. What did he mean by "heaping fiery coals" (v. 20)?

How can the gospel be our fuel for choosing grace over revenge? How can choosing grace help us and strengthen our witness?

Marriage creates opportunities for great unity but also for conflict. What practical advice for husbands did Paul offer in Ephesians 5:25-27? Give examples of ways the gospel can influence marriage in positive ways.

How can those same words apply to other relationships? How would they benefit the church?

Respond

Divide into same-gender groups of two or three people and spread out around the meeting room. This response time will help you identify key opportunities to live out part 3 of the gospel prayer in your life. Share your responses to the following questions. Then reconvene.

What's your most immediate opportunity to live out part 3 of the gospel prayer? What's the most challenging?

What's going to be the hardest part of living out grace-motivated life in these situations?

What first steps can you take this week for which we can hold you accountable? Discuss and pray for one another.

Close

In this session we focused on ways the gospel creates radical generosity toward people around us. We discussed ways a grace-motivated life is different from the motivators of guilt and greed that often burn us out and leave us disenfranchised with religion. The more we learn the gospel, the more generous we become with our resources, our time, and our relationships. We become the gospel as we rest in the gospel. Moses and the people of Israel showed this kind of generosity after they were rescued from Egypt. The New Testament church showed it when they began life together as sinners rescued by the cross of Christ. This theology of grace-motivated grace becomes very relevant to our marital, work, familial, and friend relationships. The deeper we go in the gospel, the more relevant it becomes to daily life.

Pray together.

This Week
LUKE 5-13

This week we'll return to the ministry of Jesus. Again we'll see that Christ's miraculous healings and signs point people toward the restorative nature of the kingdom of God. Here we'll see the gospel serve as the motivation for the grace-based movement that swept through the known civilization in the first century.

Consult the following reading plan to structure your Gospel reading this week. Congratulations on making it halfway through the forty-day reading plan.

This Week's Reading Plan

Day 1 Luke 6

LOVE YOUR ENEMIES

In Luke 6:27-36 Jesus teaches us how to respond to people who don't act kindly toward us. This short, nine-verse sermon contains rich wisdom on living differently than the world because we're sons of the Most High. In this passage Jesus seems to reverse justice in a way that's initially frustrating. If someone steals our coat, justice says that person should pay us back for what he took. But Christ tells us to give this person our shirt as well? Christ is flipping our worldly concept of personal retribution on its head.

Jesus, the Son of God, loved us even when we were rebelling against Him. In teaching the disciples to love their enemies, He was at the same time preaching the love God had displayed to them. He contrasted ways His followers are to act with ways sinners act in different scenarios. In each one, while a sinner has personal gain as a motive, a follower of Christ has grace as a motive. This entire message is summed up in the last two verses, in which Jesus tells us this is how sons of God act. We're to be merciful just as our Father is merciful.

REFLECT

Whom are you holding a debt over right now? In light of Christ's teaching, what would it look like to release that debt?

Who has caused you personal or professional harm? What's the forgiveness process like for you right now in that situation? What can you do to advance it?

The ability to forgive stems from understanding how merciful the Father has been to you. In your own words, record ways God has been merciful to you. Start with Jesus and go from there.

PRAY & MEDITATE

Spend a few moments asking God to give you a renewed awareness of the depth of His mercy to you. When God looks at followers of Christ, He sees them as His own children. Ask Him to allow you to have rest and confidence in that identity. With that mindset, ask Him for strength and joy to love your enemies.

Day 2 Luke 8

THE POWER

In Luke 8:40-56 we encounter a moblike scene, with crowds pressing around this man who was performing miracles and healings across the region. Notice in verse 40 that the crowds were waiting on Jesus when He returned. He was earning a reputation that drew crowds everywhere He went.

In this passage Jesus healed two people, a twelve-year-old girl on her deathbed and a woman suffering with a chronic ailment for twelve years. The little girl's father pled for Jesus to come heal his daughter when the ailing woman reached out and touched Jesus' garment, trusting that the touch would be enough to heal her. And it was! She was immediately healed. Her twelve-year condition was like a scarlet letter, labeling her unclean in society. She was an outcast. But now she was restored! Jesus made sure everyone else knew what great faith this woman had to recognize the power available in Him.

Just at the climax of joy in the story, news that the young girl had died reached Jesus. Sensing her daddy's inevitable reaction to this news, Jesus said, "Don't be afraid" (v. 50). Jesus' power wasn't bound by death. So He continued to the girl's house and asked her to get up. In an instant her life was restored.

The woman's illness and the little girl's death were curses of living in a fallen world. But Jesus was in the business of reversing the curse. The healings foreshadowed the defeat over death that Jesus would accomplish when He died on the cross and rose from the grave. You and I routinely try to deal with situations that Jesus could fix in a split second if we'd only ask and trust. When we finally come to the feet of Jesus and surrender to His power, what great healing we find!

REFLECT

How have you seen God's power change circumstances in your life? If you struggle to answer this question, here's another question for you: Have you ever invited Jesus into your life? If not, what's stopping you from doing that right now?

Do you have friends or relatives who need the power of God for their circumstances? Record their needs below and consider praying about them for a week. When you tell your friends or relatives you've been praying on their behalf, be sure to tell them about God's power to heal and restore.

PRAY & MEDITATE

Obviously, we can't physically touch Jesus today, but God has given us prayer as a means to reach out and touch Jesus. Prayer is our means of coming before the throne of grace with confidence (see Heb. 4:16) and asking our great High Priest, Jesus, to intercede before God on our behalf. Continue to pray for the friends or family you identified in the Reflect section, believing God can restore and bring hope to the situation.

Day 3 Luke 12

LOOK AT THE BIRDS

One of the greatest enemies of the Christian life is fear. Fear takes different forms, masking itself as worry, anxiety, control, overcompensation, aggression, and even racism. We all deal with fear in one way or another.

Jesus knew we'd be tempted to consume ourselves with anxiety over the tangible needs of everyday life. His response to this fear makes up the content of His teaching in Luke 12:22-34. To make a point on the extent of God's control, Jesus observed the life of a raven. Though it never prepares food for more than one meal, it still lives because God provides for it. Jesus was reminding the disciples that God actively sustains His creation. Look at the beauty of the flowers of the field, even though they do nothing to adorn themselves. God is cultivating them! Then Luke drove home the point. If God takes care of created things He simply called good when He made them (see Gen. 1:25), how much more He will take care of the human race, whom he called very good when He made it (see Gen. 1:31)!

What do we do instead of worrying? We seek the kingdom of God (see Matt. 6:33). Paul said we should "seek the things above, where Christ is, seated at the right hand of God" (Col. 3:1). In the gospel God met our greatest need—rescue from sin and death. If He did that for us, we can trust that He will be faithful to provide for us in accordance with His will.

REFLECT

What are you anxious about now? What regularly makes your mind spin with worry? List your concerns.

The gospel says the love of Christ is the antidote to anxiety. How does the truth of the gospel apply to your specific worries? Draw lines through the concerns you listed as you take them to your Heavenly Father.

PRAY & MEDITATE

Read Philippians 4:4-7. Paul provided a prescription for dealing with fear and worry. He said to live free from fear. Pray. Pray always. Pray joyfully. When you become anxious, pray with thanksgiving. Then when you cast our cares on Christ, His peace will guard you in Him. The answer to and the protection from worry is Jesus. Ask God for the peace that passes understanding to guard you and your family in Jesus.

Week 6
GOSPEL FAITH

As I pray, I'll measure Your compassion by
the cross and Your power by the resurrection.

The Gospel Prayer, Part 4

In September 1857 a movement known as the Layman's Prayer Revival began that would spark revival across the United States. A man named Jeremiah Lanphier began a prayer meeting for New York City businessmen that would meet every day at noon. Only six people attended the first meeting, but by spring more daily prayer meetings had formed across the city, and attendance swelled to ten thousand. God began saving every type of person in a movement that captivated the entire country. These men began this prayer meeting hoping for a moral recovery of America, but a full-scale salvation movement ensued among people of every class in every major city. It's believed that more than one million people were saved during this time. A group of simple laymen believed God was willing and able to send revival, and they asked God on behalf of a city in desperate need.

This same pattern takes place throughout the Book of Acts. Acts is the story of a group of disciples who believed that Jesus loves sinners as much as the gospel shows that He does. God uses the prayers of believers to unleash His power in the world. When we begin to see the gospel for everything it is, we recognize God's great compassion for humankind and His power to act on its behalf. The gospel changes the way we pray. Sometimes skepticism makes us think God doesn't do miracles anymore. Yet God is and has always been both willing and able to act for our good and His glory. He most clearly demonstrated this truth in Jesus' death and resurrection.

»» Start

What did you grow up believing about prayer, and how did you practice it? What one feature stands out most in what you were taught about prayer?

Recall some unexpected blessings in the past year. Choose one of them to share with the group. Do you think prayer may have played a role? If so, explain.

Part 3 of the gospel prayer expresses our reaction to God's love for us. We love others in response to the love we've experienced in the gospel. J. D. pointed out that the gospel motivates us to generosity not by guilt (we never give enough) or greed (we give so that we can get) but by grace (we give because we've received). The bottom line we learned is that it's impossible to really believe the gospel and not become like the gospel.

In last week's group session we learned that grace-motivated grace serves as a pattern for the way we approach relationships like marriage, parenting, work, and friendships. What a great example of the relevance of theology to our everyday lives!

As you review the past five weeks of Gospel reading, what themes or patterns stand out to you? What picture of Jesus most clearly comes to mind?

In session 6 we'll move into the final portion of the gospel prayer. J. D. will focus on ways our belief in the death and resurrection of Christ transforms our response to God's love and power. The gospel transforms the way we pray. Instead of settling for a mediocre prayer life, this session will open our eyes to the dynamic prayer life that awaits us as we tap into the stream of God's mercy. In one very important part of this session, J. D. addresses the common problem of unanswered prayer. Pay special attention to that instruction.

Watch

Watch video session 6.

As I pray, I measure Your compassion by the cross and Your power by the resurrection.

What if the compassion of God was measured by the cross, and His ability to save was measured by the resurrection?

Intercessory prayer is not informing God on behalf of someone else, but believing God on behalf of somebody else.

What if Jesus' work on earth was limited not by His unwillingness but by our unbelief?

Video sessions available at lifeway.com/gospel
or with a subscription to smallgroup.com

>>> Discuss

Use the following questions to discuss the video teaching.

How does this teaching challenge your prayer life? How does it encourage you to pray differently?

How did the section on unanswered prayer affect you? How have you dealt with God's no in the past? How do you hope to deal with difficult answers from God in the future?

Read Mark 1:40-42 and Luke 11:11-13. In Mark how can the diseased man's approach and Jesus' response be a model for the way we pray? How do they compare to your prayer life now?

In Luke 11 Jesus used the relationship between a parent and a child to teach us how God relates to us when we pray. Why would God ever say no to our prayers? Share an illustration from your own experience.

What do both of these passages communicate to us about our relationship with God when we pray? Why is the gospel critical to understanding this truth?

Now that we've seen God's response to us as we pray, let's learn more about how the Bible teaches us to pray effectively.

Read John 15:7 and 1 John 5:14-15. Both of these passages address the way we're to pray. It seems that the key to answered prayer is remaining in Jesus and letting His words remain in us. What do you think it looks like to remain in Jesus?

First John 5:14-15 tells us that if we simply ask according to the will of God, our prayers will be answered. What do you think this principle suggests about the nature of prayer?

What confidence should we have in Jesus when we pray?

Now that we've looked at aligning our prayers with God's will, let's consider the effectiveness and context of our prayers.

Read James 5:13-18. In this passage James discussed the involvement of the community of believers in our prayer lives. How does this passage challenge your current prayer life?

How should our prayer life together as the church reflect the wisdom of James 5?

James reminds us that Elijah was a mortal, flesh-and-blood man, not a fictitious character or a super-Jew. He was a righteous man who prayed in faith. Why do you think James shared this information at the end of the passage? How should this example encourage our prayer lives?

Respond

Divide into same-gender groups of two or three. Because of the nature of this week's teaching and discussion, you'll practice praying in light of the gospel. Use the guide below to pray for one another in your groups.

- Someone should share one matter for which he or she needs prayer, ideally something significant in your life.
- Someone else should volunteer to pray for the person who just shared, using the following guide.
  - —God, we see in the gospel that You're both powerful and compassionate.
  - —We know, as our Father, that You want what's best for us.
  - —We're asking for [insert shared concern], knowing that You're able to provide it and believing that You want what's best for us.
  - —As hard as it is for us, we place our hope in nothing but Jesus. Help us remain in You. Amen.
- Repeat the process until everyone has shared and prayed. Then rejoin the larger group.

 # Close

In this session we explored the anatomy of a gospel-centered prayer life. J. D. introduced the concept of intercessory faith; we don't just inform God when we pray, but we believe God on behalf of someone in our lives. We've seen that God is both compassionate and powerful in responding to our prayers. At the same time, He remains our Father who can withhold things from us for our own good. Jesus calls us to remain in Him so that we can discern His will and pray according to it. The more Christ's desires become our desires, the more our prayers become catalysts for unleashing His power in the world. Prayer is meant to be practiced in community. It should be commonplace for believers to pray for one another and to see God work miracles.

Pray together.

This Week
LUKE 14–JOHN 2

This week you'll finish reading the Gospel of Luke, encountering Jesus' radical call to discipleship and seeing an example of giving up everything to follow Him. In your reading you'll witness the death and resurrection of Christ for the third time. Hopefully, at this point some truths about who Jesus is are starting to emerge.

At the end of the week, you'll begin the Gospel of John. In this Gospel you'll find a very different style of writing from the first three you've read. Watch for the metaphors of light and darkness and what they represent in your first day of reading in John.

Use the following schedule to stay on track with this week's readings. And congratulations; you're on the home stretch of your reading sprint through the Gospels!

This Week's Reading Plan

Day 26 〉 Luke 14–16
Day 27 〉 Luke 17–19
Day 28 〉 Luke 20–21
Day 29 〉 Luke 22–24
Day 30 〉 John 1–2

Day I Luke 14

WORTH IT

Jesus had a way of recruiting followers that's counter to anything you or I would think of. Luke 14:25-33 is a great example. Let's say for a minute that we were planning to start a religion. (I know; stay with me here.) We'd probably entice people by telling them how great our religion is and the benefits it offers to those who join. We probably wouldn't start by saying they need to hate their families, give up everything they own, and carry around an execution device every day. Yet this is what Jesus laid out for the large crowds following Him.

Following Christ isn't the *easy* thing to do, but when you encounter the full power and mercy of the gospel, it becomes the *only* thing to do. Jesus made sure His audience recognized that they should count the cost of following Him just as they would in any other life-altering endeavor. He was saying we must die to ourselves if we're going to follow Him. We simply can't retain our own agendas while following Christ. Only one person can rule our lives, and that's Jesus.

Although being a disciple is tough, Jesus gives us the option to do so for our own good. He knows that the cost of following Him is worth it, because He knows that left to ourselves, we'll live an unfulfilled life. Renouncing all we have and following Christ is like letting go of the side of the pool for the first time and experiencing the freedom of swimming in the water. We can't do both. As C. S. Lewis said in his classic *Mere Christianity:*

> Fallen man is not simply an imperfect creature who needs improvement: he is a rebel who must lay down his arms.[1]

1. C. S. Lewis, *Mere Christianity,* in *The Complete C. S. Lewis Signature Classics* (New York: HarperOne, 2002), 54.

REFLECT

Jesus is calling you to lay everything down under His control. To give up everything. This is the ongoing practice of a disciple of Christ. What specifically stands out in your life that you haven't given to God and won't be easy to give to Him? Why?

Have you ever formally decided to renounce all you have to follow Christ? If so, what was it about your life that caused you to do that? If not, are you willing to do that now?

PRAY & MEDITATE

Jesus reiterated the cost of discipleship in John 12:25, in which He said someone must hate his life in this world in order to keep it in eternity. Jesus was emphasizing how much more valuable life with Him is than life as we know it with ourselves in control. Spend some time meditating on two areas of your life.

1. How have you seen the blessing of giving control to God? Thank Him for His faithfulness in that area.
2. How are you struggling to let go of control? Ask God for help from His Holy Spirit.

Day 2 Luke 21

GIVE IT ALL

Luke 21 opens with people giving money in the offering box at the temple. As rich people, one by one, gave large sums of money, Jesus suddenly fixed His eyes on the one person who clearly didn't fit in. Among the upper crust of Jerusalem's society was a poor widow. She had no standing among these men. And though the rest of the room likely did everything they could to pretend she wasn't there, we can imagine that Jesus watched her every move as she approached the offering box, dropped in two small copper coins that equal about one cent today, and moved on. Jesus stopped everything and, as He often did, began to ruffle some feathers, saying she had put in more than all of the others. She considered God worth all she had, and her generosity demonstrated her belief.

Too often we're like the rich people in this scene. Many churchgoing Christians give regular tithes, which, compared to what the rest of the world has, would be considered very large sums of money. But perhaps our motivation is to appease God, as if He were a slumlord we have to pay off so that we can go on living our lives. But here Christ was correcting our idolatry. This isn't just about money. This is about life. Are we willing to give all we have to God? Do we trust what God will do with us if we give Him all we have? This is the message of Luke 14. Christ calls us to surrender everything to Him.

REFLECT

Our spending habits reflect what we value. What does your family or personal budget demonstrate that you value?

The widow laid her life down at the feet of God. If you demonstrated a similar level of surrender, what might God ask of you?

What do you think the next step in that direction might be? What would you have the most difficult time letting go of? Why?

PRAY & MEDITATE

The gospel is the epitome of generosity. The longer we live as followers of Christ, His generosity should give rise to more and more generosity in us. Ask God to take you deeper into the generosity of Jesus so that today you can be freshly awakened to the depth of God's mercy on your behalf. Ask God to cultivate, through His Holy Spirit, a character of radical generosity in you.

Day 3 Luke 22

THE BREAD AND THE CUP

One of the most common traditions among all churches since the time of Christ is the Lord's Supper. In Luke 22:14-23 Jesus instituted this meal, which would become a staple practice for the church from that day forward. Depending on your church experience, you may have seen this ordinance practiced in several different ways. Some congregations walk forward and drink from the same cup, some pass the cup around, and some drink from individual cups. Some break the bread from a loaf, while others pass around individual crackers.

The aim of this meal was to point Jesus' followers back to His death. When He broke the bread, He said it symbolized His body, which He was giving for them. The wine reminded them of His blood that was poured out on the cross for them. Jesus was preaching the gospel to His disciples, though they didn't fully understand it yet.

This meal became a visible sermon for the church to preach and remember through the ages. By taking the elements of the meal, we declare to one another that we believe Jesus' death was for us, and we acknowledge that we've surrendered to Christ as our Savior and Lord. Together we affirm our union with Him and preach the gospel of the substitutionary death of Christ to one another and to those who don't yet believe. This is why we're to celebrate the Lord's Supper regularly with other believers.

REFLECT

Why did Jesus want the Lord's Supper to be a regular practice in church life? In what ways is it a visible sermon?

How can the practice of the Lord's Supper become not just a church ordinance but a lifestyle for you?

PRAY & MEDITATE

One central command Jesus gave as He instituted the Lord's Supper was to remember Him. He wanted this to be an occasion when distractions, fears, worries, and everything else were cast aside in order to focus on the gospel. Take a few minutes to simply remember Jesus. Remember the gospel in which you've been immersed for six weeks now. Remember His body broken on the cross and His holy blood pouring out as the payment for your sin.

Day 4 John 1

THE WORD OF GOD

The first eighteen verses in the Book of John are rich in theology. I once told a new Christian to read John 1 and be ready to discuss it with me the following week. He came ready all right—with two single-spaced pages full of questions! (From then on I decided to start with the Book of Mark instead.)

One central theme of John 1 is that this world, from the beginning until now, is about Jesus. Jesus existed in the beginning as the Word of God, He came to earth as God in the form of a man, and from Him we've all received "grace upon grace" (v. 16).

It's important for us to see the metaphor of light and darkness that John introduced in chapter 1 and used throughout the rest of his Gospel. Jesus is the Light, and darkness is the absence of the Light. Wherever Jesus isn't Lord, there's darkness.

Verse 18 leaves us with a renewed sense of the importance of following Jesus. As the only one who knows God, Jesus is the one who makes God known to us. If we want to know God, we must know Christ, listen to Him, and obey Him. Jesus and no one else (see 14:6) is the way to know God. As we get to know the character and ways of Christ, we're getting to know God Himself!

REFLECT

As you think about what you've read in Matthew, Mark, and Luke, what stands out most to you about Jesus' character?

What does this quality tell you about who God is and what He's like? Make a list of character traits, glorifying God for who He is.

PRAY & MEDITATE

John 1:12-13 tells us that by the will of God, followers of Christ have become children of God. John declared that the Creator of the world has called you His child. Spend time thanking God that in all His power, He has chosen to shower you with His grace. Thank Him for sending Jesus, God in the flesh, to give you that grace.

Week 7

SUBSTITUTE
GOSPELS

We never grow by going beyond the gospel;
we grow by going deeper into the gospel.

One year I found a new hobby: gardening. Maybe the reason I'm intrigued is that the process runs counter to our fast-paced culture. Gardening is a slow process that demands patience. If you want to eat a homegrown cucumber in July, you have to plant it in May.

Parallels to our spiritual lives abound. The care put into planting seeds is remarkably similar to the care needed for a new Christian. Constantly pulling weeds to keep plants from being choked is just like the battle we face against sin. If the plant is healthy, it grows fruit. If not, no amount of trimming or encouragement will produce a single piece.

I recently thought of another analogy. I'd been so consumed with making sure my plants were reaching the next stage of growth that I ignored the most profound connection to our spiritual lives that gardening offers: the importance of water. I can do everything right by preparing the soil, weeding, and pruning, but if the plants don't get water, they'll die. Water is their source of life. At every stage of their development, they're entirely dependent on water. Nothing else will do.

You and I so often long to get to the next stage in our spiritual development that we forget the one thing we need to survive: the gospel. The gospel isn't a stage we pass through; it's an ongoing need in our lives. No matter how mature we think we are, without the gospel we wither. If God is the soil of our growth, the gospel is our living water.

⟫⟫ Start

Have you ever grown something in your yard or known someone who has? What did you learn from the experience?

When growth hasn't occurred in your spiritual life, what factors do you think played the biggest role in your lack of growth?

Last week you studied the fourth and final part of the gospel prayer, which says, "As I pray, I'll measure Your compassion by the cross and Your power by the resurrection." In the video J. D. discussed what prayer is and ways we can easily miss the power available to us in prayer. Jesus, both loving and powerful, has given us prayer as a means to believe God on behalf of others. Sometimes God doesn't answer our prayers the way we want Him to. When He says no, we need to hold on to what we know about God's love and power as expressed in the gospel.

How has this Bible study influenced your prayer life so far?

You've studied a lot of Scripture up to this point. Has any particular story or passage stood out to you and affected the way you live your life?

In this session J. D. will confront the ways we try and move past the gospel instead of going deeper into it. We often view the gospel as the introduction to the Christian faith when it's actually the main story line of our lives. This session will show that different streams of current Christianity have moved past or perhaps diminished the gospel in some ways. In contrast, a gospel-centered church is a church in which the message of the gospel is central. It's a church that responds to the gospel in radical ways.

Watch

The good things have displaced the most important thing: what God has done for us in Christ.

What's going to grow me in Christ is knowing more about what God has done for me in the gospel.

Only being in awe of the God who gave Himself at the cross that can restructure my heart and change my passions.

I can't develop love for God in my heart just by being more committed.

The only thing that produced love for God in your heart is experiencing His love for you.

The gospel is the power of God unto salvation.

Video sessions available at lifeway.com/gospel
or with a subscription to smallgroup.com

>>> Discuss

Use the following questions to discuss the video teaching.

Which ideas in the video were you already familiar with? How have they influenced your thinking?

How does the local church you're a part of model gospel centrality? Describe a recent example, if possible.

What are some areas in which the global church could fall short of doing God's best if it isn't intentional about staying gospel centered? What role do you play in keeping the gospel central in your own church context?

Read 1 Corinthians 2:2. Did Paul actually want the Corinthians to know nothing except for Jesus and Him crucified? Why do you think Paul was so emphatic?

Galatians 6:14-15 also explores the idea that other things pale in comparison to the gospel. Paul was talking about circumcision, which had become a divisive issue in the church. Why did Paul say this subject wasn't important anymore? What are some contemporary topics that would compare to that issue?

It's often said that Sunday is the most segregated day of the week in America. How can the gospel help the modern church with racial reconciliation?

Now that we've looked at reasons the gospel is of first importance, let's consider ways we can live out these principles in our day-to-day lives.

Read 1 Timothy 6:20-21. Paul warned Timothy multiple times to guard the deposit (the gospel) entrusted to him because people would stray from the truth. How can you safeguard yourself against living for lesser goals than the gospel?

Read Galatians 3:1-3 and Ephesians 4:1. In the first passage Paul rebuked the Galatians for trying to justify themselves by what *they* did when they were already justified by what *Christ* did. Paul was so surprised that he facetiously asked who had hypnotized them. How do we slip into this same performance trap? Describe a time when this occurred in your life.

How do Paul's words of rebuke help us fight against adding to the gospel as the Galatians were doing? Try stating Paul's warning in your own words.

Read 2 Peter 1:5-9. Peter didn't think his readers had literally forgotten the cross. What do you think he meant by *forgotten* in verse 9? Describe a time when you were in a similar state.

Circle the words in 2 Peter 1:5-9 that describe supplements to our faith. What do you think is the relationship between these qualities and the gospel?

Respond

Divide into same-gender groups of two or three. For the next ten minutes discuss the statement and questions below. Be prepared to share your answers with the larger group.

> It's been said that it takes three generations to lose the gospel. One generation believes the gospel; the next assumes it; the third forgets it.

If this idea is true, what generation do you believe you're in? What can we do to ensure that we remain in and reproduce a believing generation?

Passing down the gospel to the next generation is a clear biblical mandate. How are you engaged in this practice as an individual? As a church?

What needs to happen for your life to be gospel-driven? Take time to encourage one another.

 # Close

In this session we looked at the various forms that substitute gospels can take in our lives and in our churches. We observed the significance that the New Testament places on the local church's active awareness of the gospel as its source of life. Like the early church, we can fall into works-righteousness if we're not careful. However, we shouldn't stop doing good deeds. Good deeds are a natural result of being gospel-centered. When these good deeds aren't present in our lives, though, we must be careful not to try and modify our behavior without examining our hearts. Remembering and celebrating our gospel identity is the cure for a lack of good works.

Pray together.

This Week
JOHN 3-12

In your Gospel reading this week, you'll begin in John 3, moving through several miracles Jesus performed as signs pointing the crowds to the reason He had come to earth. You'll see a division between His followers and His enemies. Jesus Himself made it clear that there's no middle ground when it comes to believing in and following Him. The dead rise, the hungry are fed, and the sick are healed.

At the end of these readings, Jesus the Messiah enters Jerusalem. The road to His death ironically began with His followers celebrating His arrival. The light and darkness metaphor will develop even more this week, so keep a close eye on John's explanations of this figurative language. You're two weeks from the end of your trek through the Gospels. Finish well!

This Week's Reading Plan

Day 31 〉 John 3–4
Day 32 〉 John 5–6
Day 33 〉 John 7–8
Day 34 〉 John 9–10
Day 35 〉 John 11–12

Day 1 John 3

THE GOSPEL ACCORDING TO JOHN

It's been worn on T-shirts, spray-painted on overpasses, printed on billboards, and displayed in countless other ways. John 3:16 is perhaps the most famous passage of Scripture in the world. We could spend hours in this verse alone, and I commend such a time of meditation and study to you.

Let's look at this verse in the context of verses 16-21. John declared Jesus' reason for coming to earth in verses 16-17. God's love for us compelled Him to save us from our sin, and Jesus was His means for doing that. Jesus wasn't here to condemn but to save. This truth is significant. If we're to model Christ, we're to tell first and foremost of the salvation He offers. Our individual lives and our churches are to be beacons of hope and mercy for others. Judgment isn't ours to declare, because as Jesus said here, condemnation is already established by what we believe about Jesus. Judgment is clear through the way we live. If we have an active love for God, it will be evident in the way we respond to the gospel on an ongoing basis.

In verses 19-21 Jesus is the light, and our sin is the darkness. When we love our sin, we run from the light because, as John's metaphor illustrates, darkness vanishes when exposed to light. So many times in life we've been afraid to let go of the sin we were enjoying because we feared God's judgment if we'd been exposed. The way to overcome this battle is to remember that there are freedom and victory in the light. Christ declares over us, "I'm here to save you, to redeem you." Our sin loses its power when exposed to the light, and we're free to live the way God created us to live. We don't live in fear of judgment but in celebration of His grace.

REFLECT

When you meditate on John 3:16-17, what does God most clearly say to your heart? Record your response as if God were addressing you personally.

If God has gone to such measures to set us free, why do you think anyone would choose to live more in fear of His judgment than in celebration of His mercy? Which of the two do you think God would rather see in our lives—fear or celebration? Why?

The church is to be a beacon of hope, mercy, and freedom in our world. How does your community perceive your local church? What can you do to improve that perception?

PRAY & MEDITATE

This whole gospel story began because the Creator of the universe loved you and me. The gospel is the account of the greatest act of love in history: God's own Son made a way to restore us to the Father and grant us eternal life with God. Spend time thanking God for His great act of love expressed on the cross and for His great power seen in the resurrection.

Day 2 John 6

JESUS IS OUR TRUE NEED

The only miracle of Jesus recorded in all four Gospels, other than the passion narrative, is a spontaneous feast He hosted on a mountain during His teaching ministry. John 6:1-15 records this miracle. What Christ taught us about Himself in this moment and in the rest of the chapter is significant. The crowd was huge—five thousand men plus women and children—and would soon be hungry. They needed to eat, yet they were on a mountain. To travel to where food would have been available would have meant the end of the day's ministry.

Never missing a teaching opportunity, Jesus first presented the problem of the food shortage to the disciples to see how they'd respond. After all, when He'd depart from the earth, these were the guys He'd leave in charge. Were they ready? Not quite. The way they saw it, the problem was too big and what they had to offer too little. Basically, they looked at Jesus and said, "We've got nothing." Jesus had them where He wanted them: helpless and ready to learn.

Jesus took a boy's simple lunch—five bread loaves and two fish—and turned it into enough food to feed everyone with twelve baskets left over. The people were so overwhelmed with excitement that they were ready to make Him their king right then and there (see vv. 14-15)!

The explanation for this miracle came in the second half of chapter 6 (see vv. 22-40). Why did Jesus do this miracle? The crowds came running back to Jesus the next day because, after all, who doesn't like free food? Instead of feeding them again, however, Jesus confronted them with the truth. He knew they wanted food that would perish, but Jesus wanted them to see their need for spiritual food that would satisfy them forever. They must believe in Jesus for their salvation. They must believe John 3:16-17. Jesus' feeding of the five thousand was a sign of His willingness and ability to bring salvation to all who call on Him.

REFLECT

Put yourself in the shoes of one of Jesus' disciples. It's late, a hungry mob is present, you're tired, and your leader doesn't appear to be worried at all. What are present-day applications to your life?

How do you tend to handle pressure-cooker moments? In what ways are you like the disciples? Different?

What's going on in your life for which you aren't yet trusting in the power of Christ?

PRAY & MEDITATE

In John 6 Christ was clearly and pointedly calling people to believe in Him for their salvation. At the same time, He was showing them His great power that was available. The same power that fed thousands would later raise Christ from the dead. That same power brings salvation to you and me. Take time to confess to God any ways you aren't leaning on His power to meet your needs. Ask Him for wisdom to understand how the gospel and the power behind it can meet your deepest needs today.

Day 3 John 12

DYING TO LIVE

The TV series called *Band of Brothers* chronicled the journey of a unit of soldiers who fought in numerous battles during the European campaign of World War II. The men had a common understanding that they were there, if nothing else, for one another. In each battle they had to entrust their lives to one another as they worked together to win.

One scene in particular stands out to me. A young soldier was having trouble going into battle. He was afraid and timid when it came time to fight. This hesitation was troublesome for the entire unit because every man needed to be fully committed to his mission. A seasoned veteran in the group took the young guy aside and explained to him what his problem was. He told him the only reason he was scared was that he didn't realize he was already dead. Once this soldier counted his life as already over, he was no longer worried about what happened to himself and could fully commit to the battle.

In John 12:20-26 Jesus taught a very similar point to His disciples. If someone loves his life here in this world, he won't be able to follow Christ. It's the simple but powerful point that you and Jesus can't both be in charge of your life. Sometimes we allow Jesus to be Lord over parts of our lives but not all. This simply won't work. When we give our whole lives to Jesus, we begin to live for eternity. Once we consider our lives over, then we can begin to truly live as God designed for us to live.

REFLECT

Dying to self-rule certainly isn't easy. In what areas of your life do you find this most difficult?

If you've already given your life to Christ, describe how this life compares to the time when you were the ruler of your life. Thank God for the difference.

PRAY & MEDITATE

Read Philippians 3:7-11. Paul said he counted everything as loss because of the surpassing worth of knowing Jesus Christ his Lord. Is this a present reality in your life? Ask God to show you more of Himself. The more you know Christ, the less you'll desire to control your own life. When you dwell in Christ, His wants and desires become yours. Ask God to cultivate in you the same attitude toward Jesus and toward self that flooded Paul's heart and mind.

Week 8
GOSPEL DEPTH

Christian growth usually isn't learning something
new but going deeper in what you already
know. Many of us know gospel doctrines,
but we've never been ravished by them.

Here we are in the final week of this eight-week journey called *Gospel*. I hope through this Bible study the gospel has stirred an awakening in your soul that has unsettled the rhythms of your life and has sparked Christ-centered transformation in you. Through the gospel God has been renovating every corner of my life, and He isn't finished yet. The deeper I go into the gospel, the more I find myself changed by it.

I hope this will be your story as well. And I hope it isn't just your story but also the story of the church. The reality is that the church is at a crossroads. In the next fifty years the church in the English-speaking world will look drastically different than it does now. Either it will continue its decline, or a new awakening will occur that will bring with it salvation and hope in a wave that hasn't been seen in three generations. I believe the latter can happen, and it will begin when we individually and corporately begin to immerse ourselves in the gospel.

This week will look a little different from the previous seven as you reflect on ways God is changing you and as you dream God-sized dreams about what you want to see God do in and through you in the future. Let this final week of study launch you on a lifelong gospel revolution!

⟫⟫⟫ Start

What moment over the past eight weeks stands out to you as a landmark for your group? Why? Describe that experience.

What role has the gospel played in major turning points in your life? What role do you hope it will play in the future? Explain.

Last week the group looked at ways we try to create substitutes for the gospel. We alter the gospel as God gave it to us to fit our wants and needs, turning God more into a butler than a sovereign King. Error, we learned, is truth out of proportion. Many movements across the Christian landscape today are guilty of taking truth out of proportion and, as a result, of leading people away from the power that resides in the gospel.

John's Gospel clearly uses a different style than the other three use. What metaphor describing Christ spoke most clearly to your mind and left an indelible impression on your heart?

This past week how did God remind you of Paul's words that the gospel is of first importance in your life?

In this final session J. D. will point to a familiar story in Scripture, the story of Jesus and Zacchaeus, to show how the gospel of Jesus creates a completely new person in us when we encounter it. This session also serves as a summary of the big ideas woven throughout the past seven sessions. The gospel, when rightly understood, overwhelms us and permanently changes us. As you listen to J. D. describe how that process has taken place in his life, consider ways Christ is changing you.

Watch

Watch video session 8.

Ultimately, the power to change comes from the acceptance that we have experienced in Christ.

We're not changed by the commands of Jesus; we're changed by an experience with the grace of Jesus.

We don't grow in Christ by going beyond the gospel but by growing deeper into the gospel.

There is literally nothing that I can do that will make God love me more. I am a son of God because of the gift righteousness of Christ and not my behavior.

The gospel is a well that the deeper in it you go, the sweeter the water becomes.

Video sessions available at lifeway.com/gospel
or with a subscription to smallgroup.com

>>> Discuss

How would you summarize J. D.'s message to the group in this final session?

You've heard and read how Jesus changed and is changing many lives. How is Jesus changing you? To which biblical figure can you best relate? Explain.

Read Isaiah 53:3-5 and 1 Peter 1:10-12. The prophet Isaiah was looking forward to the coming Messiah. Underline words that describe the Messiah. In what ways did Jesus fulfill this prophecy?

How do Peter's words help us understand the gospel that Isaiah foretold? What do you think Peter intended by introducing angels into the conversation?

Now that you've begun to understand the weight the Scriptures put on the gospel, let's look forward to how we'll now live.

Read Galatians 1:6-10. Paul emphasized that we mustn't allow ourselves to be swayed by another gospel. How can we recognize a false gospel when we hear it? How does a false gospel differ from the substitute gospels we looked at last week? Explain.

Read Acts 1:7-11. What do you think is your role in this great story of God? How can you and your church engage in this gospel mission?

Notice in verses 10-11 that the disciples were still looking up into heaven when the two men in white clothes corrected them and told them to get to work. Why do you think John included these verses? What should we glean from the angels' admonition about our own lives as followers of Christ?

How has what you've learned in this study encouraged you in your own gospel revolution? Explain.

>>> Respond

Divide into same-gender groups of two or three people each. In this final group activity you'll revisit the introductory activity you completed in group session 1. First answer the questions below. Then compare your responses to the same questions in the introductory activity in session 1. After talking in smaller groups, gather with the larger group to share a few of your responses with one another.

In your own words, what's the gospel?

Why did you become a Christian, or why would you want to?

What did you gain from this study? Share the highlights together.

If the power of God is really available to you, how do you think God is positioning your life to unleash that power in the world? What dream could you start dreaming for the glory of God in and through your life?

>>> Close

This session summarized and reemphasized the core themes expounded over the past eight weeks. J. D. showed us through the encounter between Jesus and Zacchaeus that the gospel changes everything. When we encounter Christ, we must respond. We can either reject Him or worship Him. What we can't do is ignore Him. The more we immerse ourselves in the gospel, the more God's power is unleashed in us, and the more we change into the image of Christ. As people of the gospel, we've received the power of the Holy Spirit to make this good news known throughout the world.

Pray together.

This Week
JOHN 13-21

This week you'll finish your journey through the four Gospels. The closing half of John's Gospel provides an extended look into Jesus' ministry among His disciples. He washed their feet, He promised them the Holy Spirit, He taught them a new way to live, and He prayed His lengthiest recorded prayer—all by the end of chapter 17. Once again you'll encounter the passion narrative. Reading through this account for the fourth time, you'll be tempted to skim over the words. Stay focused and allow the Word of God to sink even deeper into your mind and heart this week.

This Week's Reading Plan

THE ONLY WAY?

A few years ago one of our small-group leaders set up a meeting with me to get some advice on a bizarre scene that had taken place in his group that week. A church planter from our church who was preparing to go overseas for the rest of his life was visiting the group. He explained that he felt he had to go to this particular people group because it had never heard the gospel. As the group was taking turns asking questions about this new mission field, one woman sat troubled in the corner. Finally, after a few minutes she asked, "Do you really think they'll die and go to hell if they don't believe in Jesus? Isn't that pretty arrogant?" The church planter graciously but truthfully responded that he believed the Bible is the Word of God and that John 14:6-7 says Jesus is the only way to the Father. The woman, visibly upset, responded that such a belief is exclusive and unloving. She then left the house, never to return. What a group moment!

In John 14 Jesus made it very clear that there's no way to the Father other than through Him. Jesus told His disciples that to see Him was to see the Father! Acts 4:12 tells us there's no other name than Jesus by which people can be saved. The gospel is the way—the *only* way—to obtain salvation and restoration to God the Father. If we believe this, it changes us. It doesn't make us arrogant; it makes us humble, and it makes us active. The nations need Jesus, and as Paul said, it's our joy and mission to tell them about Him:

> *Everyone who calls on the name of the Lord will be saved.*
> *How, then, can they call on him they have not believed*
> *in? And how can they believe without hearing about him?*
> *And how can they hear without a preacher? And how*
> *can they preach unless they are sent? As it is written:*
> *How beautiful are the feet of those who bring good news.*
> **ROMANS 10:13-15**

REFLECT

If Jesus is really the only way to heaven, how should that truth affect the way you respond to Him?

In what ways can you be involved in the church's effort to reach others for Christ?

PRAY & MEDITATE

When you consider the weight of the claim that the gospel you've been studying for eight weeks is the only means of salvation, your soul will begin to ache for people who haven't heard of Christ. Pray for God to intervene and bring people in your life to salvation. Pray for them by name. Then pray for unreached people groups around the world. If you don't know of any, consult your local pastoral team or visit www.operationworld.org or www.imb.org for a list of those people groups and ways to pray for them.

Day 2 John 17

ONE PEOPLE, ONE CAUSE

Have you ever been part of a church that had trouble practicing unity, one that always seemed to find something to fight about? Don't worry; if you answered yes, you aren't alone. I've been part of three churches in my life, and two of them went through very hard periods of conflict. One of them actually split in half right in front of my eyes during a Sunday-morning service! The reality is, as long as people are involved, the opportunity for conflict will be present. Any married person will say amen to that.

Yet the church is called to be different—to stand out from the relational patterns we're used to seeing in the world. In John 17:20-23 we catch a glimpse of Jesus' prayer and plan for the church. The followers of Jesus, the church, are to be so unified that they reflect the unity Jesus has with God the Father. What a statement! Jesus and God are one and the same. This truth should be a wake-up call about the way we practice unity in our churches.

Jesus' definition of *unity* doesn't include superficial social friendships. He was talking about intertwining, interdependent lives. And then He explained why this unity is so important. It's to be the evidence to the world that God loves people and sent Jesus to save them. Do you get that? The manner in which Christians interact with one another is itself to be a witness of the gospel! In his book *The Mark of the Christian* Francis Schaeffer calls this unifying love among believers "the final apologetic" for the claims of Christianity.[1] The way we love one another speaks volumes about Jesus to the watching world.

1. Francis A. Schaeffer, *The Mark of the Christian* (Downers Grove, IL: InterVarsity, 1970), 26.

REFLECT

What, if any, disunity are you experiencing with another Christian right now (spouse, friend, pastor, church member)?

How does the gospel give you power to begin mending this disunity?

What non-Christians in your life can see the way you interact with other believers? How could you make your Christian community more accessible to non-Christians?

PRAY & MEDITATE

When we're experiencing disunity in a relationship, we tend to place the blame on the other person. Rarely do we readily admit our own faults. Before taking steps to resolve conflict, however, take time to pray and ask God to convict you of ways you've sinned against another believer. Remember, you're first a sinner; second, sinned against! Pray for God to give you the humility and confidence in Christ to forgive and to ask for forgiveness in those situations. Finally, pray for God to help you develop deeper friendships that begin to put the gospel on display for the watching world.

Day 3 John 19

THE KING OF THE JEWS

John 19, like other passages that describe Jesus' crucifixion, is intense. This passage can be divided into three clear segments:

1. Sentencing (see vv. 1-16)
2. Crucifixion (see vv. 17-27)
3. Death and burial (see vv. 28-42)

When we think about the gospel, we often focus on Jesus on the cross and forget the road He took to it. It wasn't pretty. Pilate, though finding no guilt in Jesus, sentenced Him to death. Pilate's men badly beat Him. They mocked Him and gave Him a crown of sharp thorns that pierced His head and released streams of blood that flowed down His face. He was spit on, hit, and then handed over to His accusers. Bloody and beaten, Jesus carried the heavy cross beam to the distant place where He'd be crucified. The men then took spikes and hammered them into the flesh of His hands, pinning Him to the tree.

Are you getting the picture? It's grotesque. After suffering for some time, Jesus gave up His spirit, dying by the hands of the very people He came to save. This was our Savior. Dead on a tree. His disciples then buried Him, and the tomb was enclosed with a stone and guards placed around it. It appeared to be game, set, and match. Jesus was dead, and there was no way He was getting out of that tomb.

We can't let the events of John 19 roll off our backs. We need to allow the agony to penetrate our minds and emotions. If we want to understand Christ's love, we must begin to understand His pain.

REFLECT

What emotional reaction does the pain Jesus experienced during His trial and crucifixion create in you? Why?

Jesus' death displays God's compassion and love for you. How is God cultivating in you a life of thanksgiving for the cross?

PRAY & MEDITATE

This one is pretty simple. The only way your debt could be paid was for God Himself to pay it. The payment owed was death. So God came in human form and died for you. This is the gospel message: Jesus in your place. Spend time reviewing the scene in John 19 while praising God for His sacrificial love for you. Thank Him for Jesus' death on the cross as the atonement for your sin. Worship Him for it.

Day 4 John 20

SO THAT YOU MAY BELIEVE ... AND LIVE

Chapter 20 of John's Gospel seems to have one clear goal in mind:

Jesus performed many other signs in the presence of his disciples that are not written in this book. But these are written so that you may believe that Jesus is the Messiah, the Son of God, and that by believing you may have life in his name.

JOHN 20:30-31

The point of John 20 and really of the whole book is for you to believe Jesus is who He says He is and to receive the life that comes through that belief. John wasn't writing just to inform you; he was writing to confront you with Jesus' identity—to call you to believe in Him for salvation. Notice the way verse 31 ends. With belief comes life! This is what the entire gospel revolution has been about. True gospel belief brings with it life unlike anything you've experienced before. Not only are you brought out from the death you were facing, but you also experience life as a child of God!

John 20 is filled with appearances of Christ. Jesus' resurrection declared His victory over death, and wanting His disciples to know it, He appeared to them quite a few times. Yet even more blessed are we who believe by hearing the gospel message, Jesus said in verse 29.

The purpose of this eight-week trek through the Gospels is really summed up in John's conclusion. When we believe the gospel, the more we experience the life for which we were created.

REFLECT

Jesus is still performing signs in the presence of His disciples. In what ways has Jesus displayed His great love for you lately?

What specific benefits and blessings are you taking from this Bible study (increased belief, new goals, more effective prayers, etc.)? Be sure to share some of these takeaways with others.

PRAY & MEDITATE

The resurrection changes everything. Because Jesus rose from the grave, you and I have victory over sin and death. We have new life in Him. The resurrection makes the gospel great news. This is the testimony you've spent the past eight weeks reading. Spend time thanking God for Jesus' resurrection and its implications for your life. Thank Him for ways He's changing you as a result of your time in His Word. Thank Him for the gospel and for the life you can experience because of it.

LEADER GUIDE

BEFORE YOU BEGIN

- Is there enough seating for everyone you're expecting? Will members be able to comfortably see the video from their seats?
- Is the DVD already in the player?
- Have arrangements been made to ensure everyone has or will have a *Gospel* Bible study book?
- Do you have enough pens, paper, and Bibles for participants who don't bring them?
- If needed, have you made childcare arrangements?

Session 1: Gospel Change

START (10–15 MINUTES)

Welcome everyone to the *Gospel* study and make sure everyone has a member book. Then begin the warm-up exercise.

These questions are designed to encourage everyone in the group to talk. They're subjective in nature, seeking feedback from everyone's life and experiences. Encourage multiple people to answer, but don't stall too long on these questions. The goal here is to get people to interact and perhaps laugh a little. Laughter breaks the ice like nothing else.

Lead in prayer, asking God to open hearts to the love of Christ and minds to God's truth. May He indeed begin a gospel revolution in your group!

WATCH (25 MINUTES)

Before moving into the group time, summarize what J. D. taught in the video to ensure that your group is on the same page. The key points of session 1 are:

1. Religion changes us externally by changing our behavior.
2. Religion doesn't work because it doesn't deal with our root problem of idolatry.
3. The gospel changes us internally by changing our hearts so that we desire what God desires.
4. Jesus commands us to love God, but love can't be forced. God is primarily targeting our hearts, not our behavior.

DISCUSS (25–30 MINUTES)

Review the questions beforehand and determine which ones work best with your group. Read the associated Scripture and consult a commentary, study Bible, or other study helps if necessary.

RESPOND (10–15 MINUTES)

Group members will have different answers here. There's no one right answer. Make sure everyone has a chance to answer and ensure that no one feels embarrassed giving his or her answer. If you know your group well, select a few people beforehand to share.

CLOSE (5–10 MINUTES)

At this point each week you'll want to close the group session in prayer. For this week it's OK for you and you only to pray. As the weeks progress, you'll want to give others the opportunity to pray. Model gospel-empowered prayer by praying the four parts of the gospel prayer that J. D. mentioned at the beginning of the video. Encourage group members to begin praying this gospel prayer every day in their quiet moments with God. See page 5 for the gospel prayer.

Be sure to remind everyone of the importance of Gospel reading plan (see p. 6). God's Word is indeed powerful in the life of a believer and in leading others to Christ!

Session 2: Gospel Discovery

START (5–10 MINUTES)

These questions are designed to encourage everyone in the group to talk. They're subjective in nature, seeking feedback from everyone's life and experiences. Encourage multiple people to answer, but don't stall too long on these questions.

WATCH (25 MINUTES)

Before moving into the group time, summarize what J. D. taught in the video to ensure that your group is on the same page. The key points of session 2 are:

1. Grace motivates our obedience. Paul always preceded his application teaching with doctrine teaching about the grace of God. *Therefore* is his key transitional word.
2. God doesn't accept us based on what we do. Convincing us to base our acceptance on performance is the work of Satan.
3. The more you experience the gospel in your life, the more you embody the gospel and begin to live it out. Love breeds love.

DISCUSS (25–30 MINUTES)

Review the questions beforehand and determine which ones work best with your group. Read the associated Scripture and consult a commentary, study Bible, or other study helps if necessary.

RESPOND (10–15 MINUTES)

Consider printing copies of Galatians 5:16-23 so that members can write and work with the same translation.

CLOSE (5–10 MINUTES)

Close the group session in prayer. You're encouraged this week to offer others the opportunity to pray with you.

Offer members the chance to share prayer requests. This is a great opportunity for you to connect their request to the gospel. Say something like "Given everything you heard in this session, how can we pray for you this week? How can we pray for the power of the gospel to work in your life?" Also encourage brevity in sharing prayer requests, but do so with grace.

After a few members have shared, say something like "I'm going to open our prayer time. Then if anyone would like to pray portions of the gospel prayer aloud, please do so. I'll close after a few minutes." Then pray.

Session 3: Gospel Acceptance

START (5–10 MINUTES)
These questions are designed to encourage everyone in the group to talk. They're subjective in nature, seeking feedback from everyone's life and experiences. Encourage multiple people to answer, but don't stall too long on these questions.

WATCH (25 MINUTES)
Before moving into the group time, summarize what J. D. taught in the video to ensure that your group is on the same page. The key points of session 3 are:
1. You've been made perfectly complete in Christ. There's nothing you can do to add to that identity and nothing you can do to take away from it.
2. The gospel of God's gracious acceptance of you on Christ's behalf creates in you a love for God that religion can't create.
3. Whenever God talks to believers about their sin, He first reminds them of their identity in Him (see John 8:11). Satan does the opposite. Satan takes what you've done and tries to tear down who you are.

DISCUSS (25–30 MINUTES)
Review the questions beforehand and determine which ones work best with your group. Read the associated Scripture and consult a commentary, study Bible, or other study helps if necessary.

RESPOND (10–15 MINUTES)
Consider printing copies of Colossians 3:1-4 for group members or reading the verses aloud before dividing into smaller groups.

CLOSE (5–10 MINUTES)

Close the group session in prayer. Repeat the pattern of last week, realizing that next week the group will move into an even more intense prayer time. You're encouraged again this week to offer others the opportunity to pray with you. Notice that part 1 of the gospel prayer is printed in the group session so that all members can see it.

At this point you'll again want to offer members the opportunity to share prayer requests. Please remember how significant this moment is for them. If you get nothing but awkward silence, that's OK! Don't sweat it. When you ask them to share, remember to connect the way you ask to the gospel. Here is the suggested phrasing I gave you last session: "Given everything you heard in this session, how can we pray for you this week? How can we pray for the power of the gospel to work in your life?" Also exercise grace while remembering to encourage brevity in sharing prayer requests.

After a few members have shared, open the prayer time. As you've done before, invite members to pray part 1 of the gospel prayer or for other prayer requests mentioned.

Session 4: Gospel Approval

START (5–10 MINUTES)

These questions are designed to encourage everyone in the group to talk. They're subjective in nature, seeking feedback from everyone's life and experiences. Encourage multiple people to answer, but don't stall too long on these questions.

WATCH (25 MINUTES)

If this discussion doesn't adequately summarize the video teaching, use the following key points from session 4.

1. You worship whatever you think you couldn't live without. You crave it as absolutely necessary for life and happiness.
2. The idolatry-detector test is designed to help you identify the idols in your life. Consider reviewing the questions J. D. asked.
3. We know Christ has taken all our sin, but sometimes His approval doesn't carry much weight in our lives.

DISCUSS (25–30 MINUTES)

Review the questions beforehand and determine which ones work best with your group. Read the associated Scripture and consult a commentary, study Bible, or other study helps if necessary.

RESPOND (10–15 MINUTES)

Romans 8:35-39 is an essential passage for understanding God's purpose and love for us in Christ. Make sure this section of the study receives the attention it deserves. It contains vital truths for Christian living and rich gospel application.

CLOSE (5–10 MINUTES)

Close the group session in prayer. It's time to stretch members a little in the way they pray for one another. Tell each member to think of one thing the group can pray about. Next, divide the group by gender and ask the groups to take turns sharing their requests. Here's the catch. Tell them to stick to the ABCs of sharing prayer requests: audible, brief, and Christ-centered.

This is significant. When someone shares a request, another person in the group should immediately pray for that request. That way every member will be prayed for this week. Remind groups again of the ABCs of prayer requests while praying. The goal isn't to give an eloquent prayer, because God already knows our needs. The goal is to believe God on behalf of one another. In an ideal world everyone would take a turn to pray. In reality some members aren't ready yet. Be ready to pray if no one offers to pray for a particular person. Ask someone who's confident praying aloud to do the same in the other group. You'll use this method more in the coming weeks so that members will have additional opportunities to pray and be prayed for.

Session 5: Gospel Response

START (5–10 MINUTES)

These questions are designed to encourage everyone in the group to talk. They're subjective in nature, seeking feedback from everyone's life and experiences. Encourage multiple people to answer, but don't stall too long on these questions.

WATCH (25 MINUTES)

If this discussion doesn't adequately summarize the video teaching, use the following key points from session 5.

1. Religious change is external change. We don't truly change by changing our behavior but by changing our desires. This can happen only when we embrace more of the grace found in the gospel.
2. True belief in the gospel creates a life that looks like the gospel—a life marked by forgiveness, generosity, and love in every realm and relationship we're connected to.

DISCUSS (25–30 MINUTES)

Review the questions beforehand and determine which ones work best with your group. Read the associated Scripture and consult a commentary, study Bible, or other study helps if necessary.

RESPOND (10–15 MINUTES)

Provide a means for members to record their responses so that they can share with the larger group when they reconvene.

CLOSE (5–10 MINUTES)

Hopefully at this point members are getting comfortable enough to pray with the group. Ask someone else to close the group in prayer this week. Consider approaching them before the group session to make sure he or she feels comfortable. Encouraging others to prayer lets the group hear from others and builds leaders.

Session 6: Gospel Faith

START (5–10 MINUTES)
These questions are designed to encourage everyone in the group to talk. They're subjective in nature, seeking feedback from everyone's life and experiences. Encourage multiple people to answer, but don't stall too long on these questions.

WATCH (25 MINUTES)
If this discussion doesn't adequately summarize the video teaching, use the following key points from session 6.
1. We have to understand what prayer is and what it isn't. Too often all we do is inform God about what He already knows. What if we believed our prayers are the key to unleashing His power in a specific situation and to involving us in His work?
2. Often we don't approach God with the awareness of the generosity and tenderness that He extends to us as His children.
3. When God says no to our prayers, we can still hold anyway to the love and power expressed in the gospel.

DISCUSS (25–30 MINUTES)
Review the questions beforehand and determine which ones work best with your group. Read the associated Scripture and consult a commentary, study Bible, or other study helps if necessary.

RESPOND (10–15 MINUTES)
Today try to have everyone in the group pray aloud. We've moved the prayer time into the gospel exercise to amplify the rest of this session. A guided prayer is included in this exercise that can be used by any group member who may be hesitant to pray aloud. Be sure to have large paper or a whiteboard to help with group sharing when the small groups gather again.

Session 6, continued

CLOSE (5–10 MINUTES)

Because this week's Respond was a prayer time, you probably won't want to have a second prayer time. Instead, provide a general closing word to the group about any housekeeping matters related to the next session. Encourage the group to pray for the earlier requests during the rest of the week. Ask them to check on one another for updates on the concerns they prayed about.

Session 7: Substitute Gospels

START (5–IO MINUTES)

These questions are designed to encourage everyone in the group to talk. They're subjective in nature, seeking feedback from everyone's life and experiences. Encourage multiple people to answer, but don't stall too long on these questions.

WATCH (25 MINUTES)

If this discussion doesn't adequately summarize the video teaching, use the following key points from session 7.

1. As Christians, we don't usually run from the gospel. We slowly but consistently put more weight on the effects of the gospel than we do the gospel itself.

2. The various groups mentioned aren't bad but have largely assumed the gospel and moved on to emphasize something other than the gospel itself.

DISCUSS (25–30 MINUTES)

Review the questions beforehand and determine which ones work best with your group. Read the associated Scripture and consult a commentary, study Bible, or other study helps if necessary.

RESPOND (IO–I5 MINUTES)

Provide a means for members to record their responses so that they can share with the larger group when they reconvene.

CLOSE (5–IO MINUTES)

Remind groups to utilize the ABCs of prayer requests while praying. Encourage all members to share at least one request.

Session 8: Gospel Depth

START (5–10 MINUTES)
These questions are designed to encourage everyone in the group to talk. They're subjective in nature, seeking feedback from everyone's life and experiences. Encourage multiple people to answer, but don't stall too long on these questions.

WATCH (25 MINUTES)
If this discussion doesn't adequately summarize the video teaching, use the following key points from session 8.
1. Zacchaeus is a guy who went from being one of the greediest men in the New Testament to one of the most generous. His encounter with the gospel of Jesus changed him.
2. When we encounter this gospel, it brings a complete transformation in us. We move from duty-based religion to grace-based delight in God.
3. To keep growing, we need to move deeper into the gospel, not beyond it.

DISCUSS (25–30 MINUTES)
Review the questions beforehand and determine which ones work best with your group. Read the associated Scripture and consult a commentary, study Bible, or other study helps if necessary.

RESPOND (10–15 MINUTES)
Provide a means for members to record their responses so that they can share with the larger group when they reconvene. Use this time to encourage group members to live gospel-centered lives.

CLOSE (5-10 MINUTES)

Close the group session in prayer. Because this is the last week of the study, it's fitting that you close by praying as one group together. Have a time of commissioning in which you, as the early church did with Paul and Barnabas, send out members to live in the power and freedom that come from a new understanding of the gospel. Pray that—

• members will believe the gospel in a way that creates a delight for God in them every day;
• God will begin to use them in new ways for His glory in their spheres of influence;
• they will respond to the problems they encounter with a belief in God's compassion for them;
• the gospel will continue to revolutionize their lives.

Encourage members to complete the Gospel reading plan. You might consider a party or another fellowship activity in the coming weeks to celebrate the occasion and to hear testimonies of what God is doing through your group's gospel revolution!

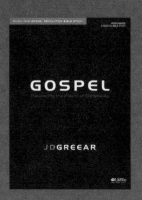

WHERE TO GO FROM HERE

We hope you enjoyed *Gospel*. Now that you've completed this study, here are a few possible directions you can go for your next one.

| REAL LIFE ISSUES | FOUNDATIONAL DISCIPLESHIP | IDENTITY |

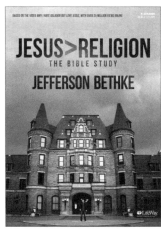

Abandon dead, dry rule-keeping and embrace the promise of being truly known and deeply loved.
(6 sessions)

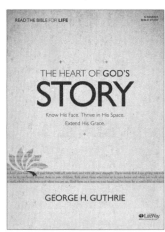

Understand why we were created, where we are heading, and how to live out the gospel in the world right now.
(6 sessions)

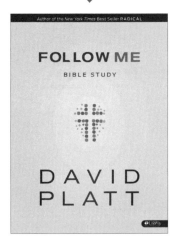

Challenge the traditions of cultural Christianity, and examine the meaning of Jesus' simple request: Follow Me.
(6 sessions)